TRADITIONAL
IRISH
COOKING

A Paperback Original
First published 1990 by
Poolbeg Press Ltd.,
Knocksedan House,
Swords, Co. Dublin, Ireland

© Biddy White Lennon 1990
ISBN 185371 092 X

Cover design by Pomphrey Associates
Typeset by Seton Music Graphics,
Bantry, Co. Cork
Printed by The Guernsey Press Ltd.,
Vale, Guernsey, Channel Islands

The Poolbeg Book of
TRADITIONAL
IRISH
COOKING
Biddy White Lennon

POOLBEG

For Honor Moore, for my husband Denis Latimer,
for Jack Hick and Jimmy O'Reilly

Their combined passions for everything that is unusual (even
unmentionable) in peasant food (from pig's nostrils to haggis)
have forced me to eat many things that I thought I hated until I
prepared and tasted them.

With one exception—none of them will ever get me to eat
tripes again!

FOREWORD

For anyone who is not a professional historian it becomes
necessary to draw heavily upon the work of historians and
other writers. I have found essential the published works of
Frank Mitchell, L.M. Cullen, Kevin Danaher, the late A.T.
Lucas and Theodora FitzGibbon. I freely acknowledge my
debt to all of them and my gratitude. It goes without saying
that any errors or misinterpretations are my own and not to be
attributed to these scholars. I have read widely and include a
full bibliography of sources where readers of this little book
may find further enlightenment and a great deal of pleasure.

My thanks must go to Fergus Gillespie, The Assistant State
Herald, for his help with the Old Irish and Middle Irish words
for food.

To Honor Moore I owe a greater debt. Without her unfailing
support and an open invitation to draw upon her vast
knowledge of food and cooking in general, and of Irish food in
particular, this book might never have progressed beyond a
project much thought about but never activated.

CONTENTS

INTRODUCTION   1

CHAPTER ONE
    Fish, Shellfish, Crustaceans and Seaweeds   7

CHAPTER TWO
    Milk and Cheese (White Foods)   29

CHAPTER THREE
    Grains, Vegetables and Fruits   47

CHAPTER FOUR
    Meat and Game   79

CHAPTER FIVE
    The Potato   117

CHAPTER SIX
    The Cup that Cheers   137

CHAPTER SEVEN
    A New Tradition   149

SOURCES   168

INDEX OF RECIPES   172

Weights, Measures and Oven Temperatures

Solid Weight Conversions

Imperial	Metric
½oz	15g
1oz	30g
2oz	60g
3oz	90g
4oz (¼lb)	120g
5oz	150g
6oz	180g
8oz (½lb)	240g
12oz (¾lb)	360g
1lb (16oz)	480g

Standards

1oz = 30g   1lb = 16oz (480g)

1g = 0.35oz   1kg = 2.2lb

Oven Temperature Conversions

°F	Gas	°C
225	¼	110
250	½	120
275	1	140
300	2	150
325	3	160
350	4	175
375	5	190
400	6	200
425	7	220
450	8	230
475	9	240
500	10	260

Liquid Conversions

Imperial	Metric	US Cups
½ fl oz	15 ml	1 tbsp
1 fl oz	30 ml	⅛ cup
2 fl oz	60 ml	¼ cup
3 fl oz	90 ml	⅜ cup
4 fl oz	125 ml	½ cup
5 fl oz (¼ pint)	150 ml	⅔ cup
6 fl oz	175 ml	¾ cup
8 fl oz	250 ml	1 cup (½ pint)
10 fl oz (½ pint)	300 ml	1¼ cups
12 fl oz	375 ml	1½ cups
16 fl oz	500 ml	2 cups (1 pint)
1 pt (20 fl oz)	600 ml	2½ cups
1½ pints	900 ml	3¾ cups
1¾ pints	1 litre	1 qt (4 cups)
2 pints (1 qt)	1¼ litres	1¼ quarts
2⅓ pints	1½ litres	3 US pints
3¼ pints	2 litres	2 quarts

Length Conversions

1 cm = 0.3 in

1 in = 2.5 cm

Recipe Notes

All cup measurements are American cups (8 fl oz)

Spoon measurements used for small quantities of solid ingredients mean gently rounded measures

INTRODUCTION

This book is an attempt to tell a story and, in the telling of that story, to make sense of Irish food traditions. The Irish have clear-cut, often trenchantly expressed, attitudes to food, drink and cooking. As a writer and broadcaster about food in Ireland I had often tried to understand and explain these attitudes as much for myself as for any audience I might have had at the time. Over the years I reached the conclusion that the only way to do this was by looking at the history of the island—the history not of battles won and lost but of its peoples, since they first began to arrive here nine thousand years ago.

I have chosen to break Irish social history into six periods, each linked to a particular foodstuff which dominated that era for particular reasons: the arrival of new settlers, climatic change, developments in agriculture, historical factors or natural disaster. Each chapter covers a different way of life, an historical period and its dominant foodstuff. I make no excuse for the fact that this is a fairly unorthodox way of approaching the subject, but it makes sense to me and, I trust, will make sense to visitors to this country in particular and to readers here with an interest in food.

This is not a history book. It is a book about food and drink with many recipes, all of which are traditionally Irish and all of which are workable and good to eat. I have concerned myself with archaeology and history only insofar as they have affected agriculture and food, and make no attempt to cover other important aspects of Irish history—cultural, political or religious. Chieftains, kings and others (be they natives or foreigners) are referred to only when their deeds had an effect upon the daily life of the people in relation to what they ate or drank. Politics and religion did have an influence in this way but, surprisingly, less than might have been imagined.

Archaeology in Ireland has made great strides in recent years and one consequence of this has been to make prehistoric Ireland more accessible, less shrouded in mystery, although many mysteries remain. It was our young son's passionate interest in archaeology which led to our tramping the hills and bye-roads of the whole island in search of neolithic sites, Bronze-Age raths, Iron-Age hill-forts, Viking settlements and Norman castles. This made me realise that an understanding of the history of the peoples of this island does not depend upon the written word. When you learn to read the landscape and grasp the importance of sophisticated dating techniques and what they can reveal about dwelling sites, artifacts, cooking sites, kitchen middens and food remains, it becomes possible to understand a great deal about how our ancestors lived. Suddenly, instead of reaching back a mere fifteen hundred years, the history of the island stretches back nine thousand years to the first settlers who reached here after the last Ice Age.

Over the years I had often wondered *why we ate what we ate:* why there seemed to be so few traditional Irish dishes served in Irish homes or in restaurants; why even excellent cooks I knew were inclined to ask: "What traditional dishes are there apart from Irish Stew, Bacon and Cabbage and Potato Soup?" There is, of course, an element of Irish understatement in that last question. This is a habit ingrained in us almost as much as the love of exaggeration. It is a feature of the Irish personality which visitors find as difficult to understand as the Irish sense of humour. I knew that there were far more traditional Irish dishes than the *famous three.* I wanted to find out what they were and why so many of them had been abandoned in favour of the *international* dishes commonly eaten in Irish homes and restaurants today.

I have a fair bit of experience of Irish homes, hotels, farmhouses, guest-houses and "digs." (There's that Irish understatement again.) In fact, my mother's work brought her all over the country and I often accompanied her as a child. When I was half-grown I became an actress and stayed in all parts of the country, north and south, during theatrical tours. Later still, as a script-writer on a radio drama serial set in rural Ireland, it was my business to keep in touch with how people lived outside the capital city where I had been born and had always lived. In all those years so little traditional food was served. Much of the cooking was just plain bad—what is known in Ireland as *lazy cooking*—three meals a day, variations on a theme of bacon and eggs, chops, steak and chips with a few tinned peas or beans thrown in for colour, and all out of the proverbial frying pan! When funds were good and I was able to afford the *better* hotels the influence of classic French cooking reigned supreme in them.

Most Irish people, it seemed to me, were not interested in good cooking. Part of this attitude is explained by an arrogance caused by the superb quality of the foodstuffs available. This led many Irish people to believe that *messing about* with good food was a custom forced on the poor foreigners by their having to disguise the inferior quality of their ingredients. In Ireland all you needed was a *plate of mate* and a dish of floury potatoes.

Because I had been brought abroad regularly as a child I knew that there was more to it than that. And even though my mother hated cooking, she loved good food. On our foreign trips, usually to France and Italy, we often acquired an Italian *au pair* who, even though she might not have been employed as a cook, would eventually end up cooking Italian dishes for us. As small children, my brother and I devoured them and yelled for more. My greatest tortures came at boarding-schools (I attended several) where I found the food almost inedible. In my early teens I resolved to learn how to cook and the family were forced to eat my experiments. Later, in my *resting* periods as an actress, I worked in various restaurant kitchens in Dublin and learnt the hard way that, even in the most expensive establishments, what the average Irish customer wanted was a good steak, the finest smoked salmon, fresh trout or crisply roasted duckling.

What emerges in this book is the fact that, while the Irish were always ready and willing to take anything they liked from foreign influences, what they ate, at any time, was largely determined by the way they were living, more usually being forced to live. It was probably fish which brought the first settlers to Ireland; it was the people's semi-nomadic, pastoral way of life which made *white meats* predominate in their diet in our *heroic* age. When the potato came along, we fell on it with relish and ate it almost to the exclusion of other foods. It was the catastrophe of the potato famines that finally destroyed what was left of the ancient way of life and the period immediately afterwards was when our older food traditions were finally lost. When, with the return of relative prosperity in the middle part of this century, we relegated the spud to an accompaniment to other foods, we had access to very little in the way of traditional recipes to fall back upon.

It is no coincidence that most *in-comers* to Ireland, particularly in this century, have, almost to a man, become involved with food production and restaurants. The German families who came here at the turn of the century, often escaping persecution of various kinds at home round Württemberg, dominate much of our sausage trade—names like Youkstetter, Hafner, Reinhardt, Herterich, Seezer, Stumps, Hick and their relatives by marriage the Capranis. Caprani is an Italian name and many Italians, most of them from Casalattico, near Rome, came here and set up a network of fish-and-chip restaurants and take-aways. Many have now opened specialist Italian restaurants. Hard on their heels came the Canton Chinese who opened restaurants all over the country. In the last few years refugees from Vietnam have come and are providing take-away foods, often from little trailers, for the plain people of Ireland.

One of the characteristics of Irish agriculture since the famine (by no means unique to Ireland and not fully explored for reasons of space later in the book), has been its concentration on the *cash crop*. Historically this is a very understandable preoccupation. But it did breed, in many country people, a corresponding neglect of the *food crop*. Very few Irish people keep even a vegetable plot. Indeed, in many parts of Ireland still, to do so would be looked down on as a sign of poverty. This is changing now but it is not all that long since there was a terrible ring of truth about the famous story told of a man

4

who was proudly telling his cronies over a pint that almost the whole of his family's Christmas dinner was home- produced—from the succulent goose (and the juicy apples for its sauce) to the floury potatoes. His friends remained totally unimpressed by this and one wit remarked: "'Tis a pity you don't live in China or you could have grown the tea as well!" Admitting that you grow your own vegetables is as likely to gain you an expression of sympathy as one of praise, even today.

Once more, however, we are being shown the way by in-comers. Ireland was a favourite settling place for many of those *drop-outs* from the late sixties and seventies seeking *the good life*. It is interesting to see just how many of these people, with Dutch, German and other European names, are now involved in the growing farm-cheese movement, in organic vegetable-growing enterprises, and in various other ethnic, specialist, or health-food shops.

To the visitor, the restaurants in our cities and towns must seem to be dominated by international fast-food chains and the shelves of our supermarkets to groan under the weight of imported processed foods. Many housewives in Ireland today are more likely to make a good attempt at a *pizza* or a *chow mein* than a traditional Irish dish.

But all is not lost. Traditional Irish food is alive and well and growing in status once more. I hope the recipes in the last chapter of this book, which have been contributed by the chefs of some of our finest restaurants, will encourage you to seek out and demand Irish food in our hotels and restaurants. Good eating!

CHAPTER ONE
FISH, SHELLFISH, CRUSTACEANS
AND SEAWEEDS

The history of man in Ireland begins about nine thousand years ago in the period called The Old Stone Age. This, in terms of Ireland's geological history, is a very short time ago. The very best expression of this was given by G. L. Herries Davies in a radio talk a few years ago. He likened the history of the earth to the 220-km journey from Eyre Square in Galway to O'Connell Bridge in the centre of Dublin. Each kilometre of the journey represented 21 million years of earth history. On this scale Ireland did not actually appear out of the ocean's depths until a traveller from Galway to Dublin had reached Islandbridge on the outskirts of Dublin, roughly where the Phoenix Park and Heuston Railway Station are today. The whole history of man in Ireland takes up only the width of a kerbstone on O'Connell Bridge.

Man arrived in the wake of the retreating ice of the last Ice Age. He came in search of food. As soon as the ice had begun its retreat about a thousand years before, the open tundra which had covered Ireland (rather like the winter fastnesses of Greenland and Siberia today) was slowly replaced by invading plants and trees. Pine and hazel were the dominant trees but there were junipers, willows, oaks, elms, birches, alders and ash trees as well. Animals and birds followed the plants and men followed them. These early settlers had no knowledge of farming. They were hunters and gatherers. They did know about edible nuts, berries, plants and roots and, more importantly, they had discovered the seasonal movement of wild animals and fishes. They hunted these with a primitive harpoon-like tool made from a microlith, a tiny flint blade, set in a bone or wooden handle.

From archaeological examination of their settlements, particularly their kitchen middens, a tentative reconstruction of their lifestyle has been advanced which suggests that they did not roam aimlessly over the island but moved between three or four campsites in a yearly pattern which was governed by the seasonal migrations of fish, birds, animals, and the seasonal availability of plants, seeds, nuts and berries.

Early spring found them camped on the coast near the estuaries of rivers where they harvested and ate shellfish (oysters, mussels, periwinkles, cockles, limpets) and seaweed. Here they could catch inshore fish (tope, cod, ling, mackerel and sole), nesting seabirds and their eggs (auks, puffins), and the first run salmon.

In summer they followed the salmon up river to the lakes where they also caught other fish and harvested fruits and berries. There were large stocks of eels in the lakes as well but these were easiest to catch as they began to shoal to go downstream again in the autumn. They probably followed the eels down into the river valleys in the autumn and set up their winter camps well above the flood plains of the rivers. At this time they harvested wild hazelnuts which were an important winter food and widely available in the forests.

During the winter they hunted and trapped game and wildfowl. Wild pig seems to have been the most important source of meat, along with hare and the occasional red deer. They ate birds too (pigeon, duck, red grouse) and a bird of prey, a goshawk, may have been used for falconry rather than food although this is pure speculation. While archaeological excavation can tell us a great deal, it cannot tell us everything. We do not know, for instance, how they cooked their food. They had no pots that we can discover so that we guess that much of their food was eaten raw or cooked over an open fire.

Some time after these earliest settlers arrived, a second group came to Ireland. They had stronger, heavier tools with which they began to create the first small clearings in the forests and they possessed pronged spears and perhaps even fish-hooks. It has been suggested that the smoking of fish, particularly eels, for consumption during the winter began during this second stage of colonisation of the island.

It is fascinating that the foods most favoured in Ireland today were among the very first foods eaten in the country—the salmon and the pig—and that those most in demand for export from Ireland to Europe now were a major source of food then—oysters, mussels and eels. The importance of the salmon can still be clearly seen. If a countryman in Ireland today asks an angler if he has caught a "fish," he does not mean any old fish but, specifically, a salmon.

Not all the tall tales associated with the salmon are fisherman's stories. Many of them are *piseogs* (superstitions) or mythical tales or fables. In the Irish sagas a king called Fintan is said to have escaped The Flood by being changed into a salmon. While swimming under a hazel tree, the Tree of Knowledge, some nuts fell from the tree into the water hitting the salmon on its back. This not only gave the salmon its spots but transferred the tree's knowledge to the salmon, known ever after as the Salmon of Knowledge. Finn MacCumhaill, the legendary leader of a band of heroic warriors called The Fianna, while still under instruction as a warrior, caught the salmon and was set to cook it for his master. While he had it set before the fire he saw a blister rise on its skin. He burst the blister with his thumb, burning his thumb in the process. As he sucked on his thumb to cool it, the salmon's knowledge passed to Finn causing him to be elected leader of the Fianna amid great feasting and celebration.

In Ireland today festivities are still associated with fish and shellfish. The most famous festival is held in September to celebrate the Galway Oyster. People gather from all over the world for a week and consume tons of oysters washed down by lakes of stout. Wexford Town still has its Mussel Festival when tons of locally farmed mussels are washed down by—yes, you guessed! —rivers of stout and a small wine-lake. This consumption of wine perhaps reflects the town's historical status as a place where foreigners held sway, from the Vikings to the later, French-speaking Normans. Midsummer's Day in Ballintrae, Co. Antrim was once the scene of a Salmon Dinner held by salmon fishermen to celebrate the start of the summer fishing season. The menu was always a fish soup followed by salmon washed down with Bushmill's Whiskey from the oldest distillery in Ireland and still a brand with a high reputation.

Today Irish fish and shellfish are recognised as being of the very highest quality, much sought after by tourists and our European neighbours, and exported in vast quantities. The Irish people themselves have a curiously ambivalent attitude to them, however, and eat relatively little fish. This is largely explained by the fact that we have a serious distribution problem within the country; the catch often reaches the Paris fish-markets before it is available in Irish towns and it never reaches most villages. But there is another, historical, reason.

Christianity may have brought many benefits to Ireland but it also established in the Irish psyche the concept of fish as a *penitential* food, the fish of *fasting days* and Fish Fridays. From early Christian times until relatively recently the long fasts of Lent and Advent and other Holy Days of Obligation scattered throughout the year meant that for long periods the vast majority of the population were obliged to abstain from eating meat. Thus fish became the despised food of denial and penitence instead of being celebrated as the food which first brought men to Ireland and the dominant foodstuff during this whole early period of our national history.

But being Irish, we have festivals to celebrate that fact too. Until quite recent times numerous towns and villages all over the country celebrated *The Whipping of the Herring* on the Saturday before Easter. To mark the end of the Lenten fast a herring was threaded onto a rod and a crowd of lads, often the butchers' apprentices, whipped the herring through the streets of the town with long rods. In some towns the final indignity inflicted on the herring was to *drown* it!

Salmon

Today's Irish salmon can be either wild salmon or farmed salmon. The farmed variety is of good quality but is quite different in texture and taste to the wild fish, whether cooked fresh or eaten smoked or pickled. True wild salmon is available for a limited season (January - September) and never in real quantity except for short periods when there can be a glut on the market. Farmed salmon can be purchased all year round. Consequently, the price of the wild salmon is significantly higher than that of the farmed variety, except during those short periods of glut.

The ancient Irish more than likely cooked the larger fish on a spit over an open fire, thrusting a stick down the full length of the fish from mouth to tail and binding pliable willow rods to the outside of the fish with grasses and reeds to hold it together during cooking. In Co. Kerry, I have seen a whole salmon laid on the ashes of an open fire, wrapped in several layers of wet newspaper, and covered with another layer of hot ash and embers. It was left until the paper was com-pletely dried out. At that point the flesh was perfectly cooked. Today it can be simpler to barbecue a medium-sized fish using a hinged fish-grill.

Barbecued (Whole) Salmon

1 whole salmon (approx. 3.5 kilos)

for basting:
2 oz melted butter
3 tbsp honey
or
juice of 2 lemons
freshly ground black pepper

Melt the butter and mix in either the honey or the lemon juice and the black pepper. Place the salmon in the hinged fish-grill and brush on both sides with the butter mixture. Cook it over charcoal for about 40 minutes, turning and basting it frequently. While the butter/honey mixture is the more tradi-tional Irish baste, the butter/lemon juice mixture might be more suited to modern tastes.

This method can be used with other fishes like large trout, pike or even mackerel. Adjust the cooking time to suit the size of your fish. The traditional accompaniment with summer salmon is today's new potatoes, that is, freshly dug, tiny new potatoes. A green salad containing sorrel leaves as well as lettuce would be both traditional and tasty.

Baked (Whole) Salmon

> 1 whole salmon (approx. 3.5 kilos)
> aluminium baking foil (enough to completely
>   envelope the fish)
> 2 oz melted butter

Weigh your fish. Take a piece of continuous foil large enough to wrap the salmon into a loose parcel. Brush the inner surface of the foil with melted butter or vegetable oil. Place the parcel on a suitable baking dish and cook it in a pre-heated oven at medium temperature (165°C, 330° F Gas Mark 3) for 25 minutes per kilo. If you are serving the fish hot allow it to stand, still wrapped, outside the oven for 10 minutes before serving. If you wish to serve it cold then allow it to cool completely before removing its wrapping. Individual salmon steaks (2 cm thick) can be cooked this way—cooking time 20 minutes.

Accompaniments for Salmon

The traditional Irish garnish for salmon, whether the fish is served hot or cold, is either watercress or sorrel leaves. Nowadays, in restaurants, it would be almost inevitable that a hollandaise sauce would accompany hot salmon and mayonnaise the cold fish. Why not get back to a more traditional flavour with the following recipes?

Green Mayonnaise

> 1 cup mayonnaise
> 4 tbsp (mixed) fresh leaves of sorrel and watercress

Remove the stems from the leaves of the sorrel and the watercress. Blanch the leaves for 2 minutes in boiling water. Refresh them under cold water from the tap and then drain them well. Chop the leaves very finely. Stir the chopped leaves into the mayonnaise. This last step can be accomplished using a food processor to get a really smooth green sauce.

Cream and Sorrel Sauce

> 1 cup fresh cream
> ¼ lb fresh sorrel leaves
> 1 oz butter

Remove the stems from the sorrel leaves and blanch the leaves for 2 minutes in boiling water. Drain them well and chop them finely. Melt the butter in a small enamelled or stainless steel saucepan, add the chopped sorrel and cook it in the butter until it has reduced to a purée. This will take about 4 minutes. In another saucepan bring the cream to a boil, add the puréed sorrel and butter, bring back to the boil and season with a little salt and freshly ground black pepper. Serve very hot.

Smoked Salmon

Prized by the native Irish and by visitors alike, the very finest smoked salmon is still fresh wild fish cold smoked over smouldering oak wood. Less expensive and, it should be admitted, different in flavour and texture, is the farmed smoked salmon which is increasingly available.

We eat smoked salmon plain, in paper-thin slices, with a squeeze of lemon juice and a pinch of paprika, accompanied by good brown bread and butter.

Sea, White, Salmon Trout

As the name implies, this fish is a sea-going trout and is considered a great delicacy—a "run" of sea trout is well worth waiting for by both fisherman and cook. The fish can vary in weight between half a kilo and two kilos. The larger fish are treated exactly like salmon and the smaller ones like trout.

When smoked, sea trout has a subtle, more delicate taste than smoked salmon, and is usually served in small fillets to be eaten with brown bread and butter. It is quite common for pungent, creamed horseradish sauce to be served with smoked trout but I think this is more suitable for the more robust taste of smoked mackerel, as it tends to overwhelm the trout.

While it is perfectly simple to make this sauce by adding 2 teaspoons of freshly grated horseradish root to a half-cup of thick whipped cream, Irish cooks tend to cheat and use a commercially prepared creamed horseradish sauce added to fresh cream.

Eels were a very important food from earliest times in Ireland. However, it has to be admitted that eating eels, as opposed to exporting them to Europe, has gone out of favour. Like many foods which were popular before the potato famine they came to be despised as a food of the poor. This is a great shame.

The first Irish farmers in neolithic times, some of whom lived on artificial lake-dwellings *(crannogs)*, used a type of eel-spear which was still in use until relatively recent times. Eels were also caught in long conical nets almost identical to those still used today on the River Bann and Lough Neagh which is one of the largest silver eel fisheries in Europe. River fishing for eels was once important, sometimes with baited lines, but often with weirs built from stone and wattles. In the 17th Century there were 22 recorded weirs on the Shannon at Athlone.

Eels were eaten fresh but they were also salted and stored, like herrings, for winter use. Eel fat was considered a cure for rheumatism and the skin used as a charm against rheumatic pains. Today, when it is served, it is most likely to be smoked eel included in a mixed seafood platter. If you can buy smoked eel, skin it and remove the fillets from the central bone. Eel is very rich and a four-inch piece is quite sufficient for anyone as a starter.

Lough Neagh Fried Eels

2-2½ lb silver eels (skinned and cleaned)
2 tbsp seasoned flour
oil or fat for frying

This was the traditional way of cooking the young eels of the loughside eel-fishermen, according to Florence Irwin who collected many recipes from this part of Ireland. It works best with silver eels, the very young elvers, or with smaller mature fish which must be beheaded and then skinned and cleaned.

Place the dressed eels into a pot of cold water which is then brought to a boil and allowed to simmer for 3 minutes. Drain the eels and then dry them well. Toss them in flour seasoned with salt and freshly ground black pepper to which a pinch or two of ground paprika may be added. Deep fry the eels until brown and crisp. Serve with lemon juice and good wholemeal bread. Eels are a rich, oily fish and this amount would serve 6 people.

Herring

If salmon was, and to a certain extent remains, the food of kings and the embodiment of all things good, then the poor herring languishes at the bottom of the fish hierarchy today— the fish of penitence, of the poor—unloved and unwanted by many. Not many years ago when the European Community enforced a herring fishing quota to allow breeding stocks to replenish themselves there was an outcry in most northern European countries. It went almost without notice in Ireland.

Despite our current lack of regard for the humble herring it was in past times the fish most commonly eaten by the mass of the Irish people. There are more recipes for the despised herring than for any other fish. Always a fickle fish, the herring shoaled unpredictably and fishermen often had difficulty finding the herring grounds. The introduction of new technology in this century has resulted in a dramatic decrease in stocks from overfishing. The herrings shoal in Irish waters in September, hence the name harvest herrings.

The great days of the salt herring were during the 18th and 19th centuries when the basic diet of potatoes cried out for a *tasty relish*. The herring was in great demand not just round the coast but inland, and vast quantities were salted down in barrels for winter use. Fresh herrings were eaten too, but unless they are sea-fresh they are better salted, pickled or smoked. They were preserved by close-packing them in the barrels between layers of salt. They were removed as needed and soaked overnight in water. It was quite common for them to be simmered, for about 10 minutes, along with the potatoes which they were to savour. Ling, mackerel and eel were salted in much the same way.

Killybegs Herrings

   12 fresh herrings (filleted)
   1 tbsp melted butter
   3 carrots
   4 onions
   3 cloves of garlic
   3 tbsp fresh chopped parsley
   2 cups of ale or beer
   ¼ cup wine vinegar
   1 bay leaf
   4 whole peppercorns
   1 sprig fresh thyme
   4 whole cloves
   salt and freshly ground black pepper to taste

Wash and thoroughly dry the fish. Brush the butter all round the inside of a large oven dish. Chop 3 of the onions and the carrots, parsley and garlic and spread evenly over the base of the dish. Add the sprig of thyme, the whole spices and the bay leaf. Pour over half the ale or beer and bring it to the boil. Turn down the heat and simmer until the vegetables are tender. Slice the remaining onion into thin rings. Lay the herrings in a layer over the vegetables and spread a layer of onion rings on top of them. Add the wine vinegar and enough ale just to cover the fish. Bake in a pre-heated fairly hot oven (200°C, 400°F Gas Mark 6) for 20 minutes. Remove from the oven and allow to cool in the dish. Serve cold with fresh soda bread to mop up the gravy. As a starter this would serve 12 people, or 6 as a main dish.

Fried Herrings in Oatmeal

This is a classic, traditional dish eaten all round the coast and anywhere else that fresh herrings are to be found. The flaked oatmeal gives a crisp outer coating with a delicious nutty taste. Herrings can vary greatly in size so you must judge how many fish you need by eye.

    4-8 herring fillets (1 large or 2 small per person)
    8 tbsp (heaped) oatflakes
    4 tbsp melted butter
    2 beaten eggs
    3 tbsp flour (heaped)

Wash and thoroughly dry the herring fillets. Dip each fillet into the flour, then into the egg, then into the oatflakes, making sure that it is completely coated in each. Press the oatflakes well onto the surfaces of the fish so that it adheres. Melt half of the butter in a large, heavy-bottomed frying pan and heat it until it just begins to foam. Put in the fish and cook on one side, over a medium heat, until the oatflakes are evenly browned (not burnt). This will take about 4-5 minutes. Turn the fish fillets over to cook on the other side. If your pan is not large enough to cook all the herrings at once the first batch may be kept warm in the oven until the second batch is cooked. You may need to add more butter as you turn over the fillets. The amount of butter you need will vary depending on the oatflakes.

In the old days, it would have been exceptional for eggs to be used to coat the fish. The herrings would have been dipped in milk before coating with the oatflakes. It is slightly more difficult to get the oatflakes to adhere to the fish this way but it can be done.

Serve with sprigs of fresh parsley and a wedge of lemon. This is not traditional but is almost always done today. Good brown bread and butter to accompany or beautiful floury boiled potatoes with butter go best with this marvellous fish.

Mackerel

Another fish which shoals seasonally round the Irish coasts, often coming right in to the piers and harbours. Many a young lad has got his first taste for fishing hanging over the harbour-wall of a summer evening pulling in scores of greedy, gaudy mackerel. In winter the shoals retreat to deep water.

On one thing everyone agrees, mackerel must be eaten almost as soon as they are caught to be at their best. They are fat, oily fish and deteriorate rapidly. In recent times they have become a very popular hot-smoked fish (a method which cooks the fish as it smokes). They are nearly always served with a strong, sharp sauce which cuts through the oily taste. Traditionally this would be rhubarb, gooseberry or creamed horseradish sauce. Grill the fillets, brushed with melted butter, under a hot grill for about 5 minutes each side, or pan fry them.

Gooseberry Sauce

½ lb gooseberries
3 fl oz water
2 level tbsp caster sugar
1 oz butter
1 tbsp fresh chopped fennel leaves

Cook the gooseberries in 3 fluid ounces of water, along with the sugar, butter and fresh fennel, until the berries slit and pop open.

A member of the cod family, ling was a staple food along the western seaboard of Ireland where it was filleted, then dried and salted for storage. Because I was born in the heart of Dublin, on the east coast, I was unaware of its existence until well-grown. I then read a eulogy to the magical properties of ling by Kerry playwright, publican and enthusiastic eater of all things Irish, John B. Keane. I went in search of this wondrous food which was "good enough to sole your boots with." I found nary a trace of it in the fishmongers of Dublin. Just recently, however, it has begun to appear in the shops, presumably as Irish people who have spent holidays in Spain and Portugal acquire a taste for the wonderful salt cod dishes of those countries. This is its main use. It can be substituted for salt cod in any recipe.

Boiled Ling

1-1½ lb salt ling
1 onion (sliced)
1 cup milk
1 cup water
1 tsp cornflour
freshly ground black pepper

Cut the salted ling into 4 equal portions and put to soak overnight in a pot of cold water. The next day, drain the fish and place it in a pot with the milk, water and the sliced onion. Bring it to the boil, turn down the heat and cook at a simmer for 30 minutes. Take up the fish portions with a slotted spoon and keep them warm. Season the sauce with freshly ground black pepper to taste. Now thicken the sauce with the cornflour, mixed with a small amount of cold water. Pour the sauce over the fish and serve with a dish of boiled, floury potatoes and butter.

Shellfish

In Dublin's fair city,
Where the girls are so pretty,
I first set my eyes on sweet Molly Malone.
She wheeled her wheelbarrow
Through streets broad and narrow,
Crying, "Cockles and mussels, alive, alive, oh!"

This old Dublin street song gets right to the heart of the matter—if your shellfish are not alive, alive O! when you start to cook them you should not be eating them. As we have seen, it was probably the rich harvest of shellfish round our coasts which encouraged the first settlers to come here and down through the centuries the Irish have eaten, with every sign of enjoyment, every available mollusc: clams, winkles, whelks, limpets, cockles, scallops; but the most commonly enjoyed today, as in the past, are oysters and mussels.

Oyster

Oysters were once far more plentiful than they are today (even now that we export most of our annual crop), and used to be shipped round the country in barrels. They were very cheap and even looked down on as fit only for the poor. It was usual then to cook oysters in pies and stews but it should be said that they toughen and become rubbery if cooked for very long and the modern taste for raw oysters probably provides the best way to enjoy them.

Oysters are prised open with a special, short-bladed knife. This requires considerable practice and is an admired skill. At the oyster festivals which are held to celebrate the opening of the season there are oyster-opening competitions in which the judges look not just for speed but for the presentation of the oyster. Oysters are served from the half-shell, usually on a bed of crushed ice, and sprinkled with a dash of lemon juice, sometimes a splash of tabasco. The classic accompaniment is stout.

Mussel

This is the commonest shellfish on sale here today. If you know where to go it is still possible to harvest them wild but they are extensively farmed. The technique for doing this is credited to an Irishman called Walton who was shipwrecked in the Bay of Aiguillon, just north of La Rochelle on the western coast of France, in 1235. To help himself survive he invented a net attached to long poles sunk into the mud-flats. This was to catch birds, mark you! We do not know how successful he was with the birds but he discovered that the poles became covered with mussel spawn and young mussels grew on them in abundance. Being an Irishman with an eye to the main chance he abandoned bird-netting and went into mussel farming. To this day the Bay of Aiguillon is full of stakes.

Today the mussels are most commonly farmed by suspending ropes from rafts. This method keeps the mussels away from predators, less sand invades their shells (which makes them easier to clean and prepare) and they grow bigger than the truly wild variety. They are plump and tasty and can be harvested very easily. Unlike farmed salmon, which is sometimes rejected by gourmets as second-best, farmed mussels are well thought of.

There are two principal ways of preparing mussels: the older way—with milk or cream to make a rich soup—or with wine or a light beer or cider. Today in restaurants, there is a vogue for serving them in the half-shell with garlic butter and lots of brown bread to mop up the juices but this, however delicious, is not a particularly Irish way with mussels.

Mussels with Wine

48 mussels
1 cup dry white wine
2-4 cloves garlic
1 onion
1 tbsp butter
1 handful fresh chopped parsley
salt and freshly ground black pepper to taste

First choose your mussels very carefully, even if it means falling out with your fishmonger. The shells should be either tightly closed or, when given a sharp tap, they should close promptly. This means that they are definitely alive-O!

Now scrub the shells thoroughly with a hard brush and remove the beards—the tuft of fibres projecting from the shell which anchored the mollusc to its underwater perch. Place the mussels in a large pot. They used traditionally to be put in with some sea-water but, in fact, no liquid is necessary at this stage. Place the pot over heat with a lid. The mussels will steam themselves open in the water clinging to the shells. This takes only a short time. When the shells are all open (discard any which have remained closed) remove the top half-shell. Do this carefully over the cooking pot so that any juice which escapes is caught. Put the mussels in the bottom half-shell aside into a dish over a steamer so that they are kept warm. Melt the butter in a pot and soften the finely chopped onions and garlic in it. Add the wine and allow it to bubble for a while and reduce. Now tip in the mussels and their juice and leave them just long enough to warm through. Serve them quickly sprinkled with the chopped parsley. Mussels become tough very quickly from over-cooking so do not be tempted to reduce the wine while the mussels are in the pot. Lots of good brown bread to mop up the delicious soup. Drink the rest of the wine with them or drink stout.

Carrageen Winkles

Carrageen is an edible seaweed and the one still commonly in use in Ireland today. Apart from its properties as a gelling agent it is widely used in the manufacture of ice-cream, beer and medicines. Considered a valuable invalid food, it contains iodine and other mineral salts. It was, and still is, the traditional cure for chesty coughs and bronchitis in children. Many the bowl of carrageen blancmange I downed as a child and, in his turn, my own son was given it —disguised in milk-shakes!

When gathered fresh, during April and May, it is brown and must be washed to get rid of the salt before it is bleached and dried. This was always done by spreading it out on the grass near the seashore and covering it with a fishing-net to stop it blowing away. After several dowsings in fresh water or good Irish rain it was allowed to dry and the stalks trimmed away before being stored in a dry place. Thankfully, it is now freely available, ready to use, either as a medicine or as a *kitchen*. This is a dialect word which you may come across. Long ago, it meant a tasty morsel to be chewed, or something to be cooked, as a savour, with potatoes. Small amounts of fish (usually salted), seaweed, bacon, and even buttermilk, were often referred to in this way.

Any of the smaller shellfish—cockles, winkles, whelks, even mussels and small scallops—can be used for this unusual recipe. I have been served it in West Cork and in Kerry made with a mixture of all of these. The worst part of the preparation is taking the molluscs out of their shells when they have been cooked. Bent pins, or a steel crocket hook, definitely required.

½ cup dried carrageen
2½ cups water
2½ cups milk or cream (or mixed)
2½ cups cooked (shelled) shellfish
   (a mixture of cockles, winkles, etc.)
salt and freshly ground black pepper

Cook the carrageen in the water for 30 minutes. Most of it will have disintegrated but you can pass any larger pieces through a mouli-sieve. Add the seaweed and liquid to a pot with the milk or cream and simmer it for 10 minutes. Add the flesh of the shellfish and the seasoning and bring just to boiling-point. Eat it at once as a delicious fish soup with lots of brown soda bread.

Sloke or Sea Spinach

A seaweed found all round the coast of Ireland, it is traditionally served as a vegetable with both fish and bacon; less often, and less widespread, with lamb which has been grazed on sea-grass pastures. In late 16th and 17th century Dublin they had special silver pots for it. It requires very long cooking—4 to 5 hours—and can be preserved in earthenware crocks.

2 lb sloke
1 tbsp butter
juice of ½ lemon
1 tbsp cream

Wash the sloke well to remove all traces of sand and cut away any fibrous stems. Cover with water in a large pot and bring to the boil then simmer for 4-5 hours until it is tender. Drain thoroughly, chop roughly and mix in the butter, cream and lemon juice.

Dillisk or Dulse

Found mainly on the west coast of southern Ireland and more particularly valued in Ulster, dillisk is another edible seaweed which requires long cooking. It can be prepared in much the same way as sloke in the previous recipe but needs a preliminary soak in water for about 3 hours. It can be cooked in milk for 4-5 hours and is occasionally served chopped and mixed through boiled, mashed potatoes.

Dublin Bay Prawns, Lobsters, Crayfish and Scallops

These are all luxuries in Ireland today. A current joke in Dublin is that "You would need to be a lawyer to afford lobster." We export all of these seafoods in large quantities to the capitals of Europe. It is one of the greatest frustrations of travelling round Ireland to see lobster-pots and creels on every small country pier—but try to buy a lobster! They are usually available in the more expensive restaurants—those frequented by lawyers? It has gone so far that a variation of the prawn recipe below, one using lobster meat which has been extracted from the claw before cooking (now that is a tricky operation), is called *The Dublin Lawyer*.

Dublin Bay Prawns flamed in Irish Whiskey

This is definitely the only recipe in this book which will waste Irish whiskey. (There are far better ways of using it. Like drinking it.) Let us dispose too of another of those hoary myths. The Dublin Bay Prawn is not unique to Dublin Bay. It is actually a widely distributed species known as Norway Lobster *(Nephrops Norvegicus)*. The name arose from the fact that the prawns came from fishing-boats which had been forced to take refuge in Dublin Bay from storms in the Irish Sea and were sold by women in the streets of Dublin.

2½ lb whole fresh prawns (if using fresh,
　　pre-cooked, shelled prawns then 1 lb is enough)
2 tbsp butter
4 tbsp Irish whiskey

for the sauce:
2 onions
1 large clove garlic
2 tbsp butter
½ cup cream
½ cup fish stock (use the water in which you cook the prawns)

If you are using fresh, uncooked, whole prawns (preferably still alive) then drop them into boiling salted water (to cover) for 10 -15 minutes. Retain a half-cup of the cooking water to use as stock if necessary. Remove the flesh from the tails of the prawns and set it aside.

To make the sauce, first melt the butter in a saucepan, add the peeled and finely chopped onion and garlic and cook them gently until softened but not browned. Add the stock and turn up the heat until it reduces to about one third its volume. Add the cream and cook briskly until the sauce thickens. Season to taste with salt and freshly ground black pepper.

Just before you are ready to serve the dish, melt 2 table-spoons of butter in a wide heavy-bottomed frying pan. Add the prawn tails, turn them quickly until they are just warmed through. Warm the whiskey and pour it over the prawns in the pan, setting it alight with a match. (Careful! A second pair of hands is invaluable at this point. Irish people seem to have a gift for doing this. Perhaps the trick is to have drunk a fair amount of the whiskey while preparing the sauce?) Add the flamed prawns to the hot sauce when the flames have died away. A quick stir and serve at once. I still think it's a waste of whiskey.

CHAPTER TWO
MILK AND CHEESE (WHITE FOODS)

The second distinctive settlement of Ireland was by groups of semi-nomadic farmers who arrived about six thousand years ago. We do not know where they first landed in this country or whether they reached Ireland from Britain or continental Europe. It seems likely that they arrived in small boats made of skins stretched over wood, craft not unlike the curraghs which can still be seen in the west of Ireland.

They were probably preceded by advance parties in search of flint deposits and elm-rich woodlands which they would have associated with fertile soils. They needed the flints to make the axeheads with which they cleared woodlands but, because they still relied upon hunting and gathering to supplement their diet, they would have been attracted by a richly wooded land which was still sparsely populated. The main parties would have brought with them plants and animals unknown in Ireland; species and breeds very different to those we know today which belonged to the older civilisations of the east. The early horse (no bigger than a pony), mountain sheep, small cattle (predecessors of the Kerry cow we know today), the cat and the dog, were early introductions.

They would have cleared small areas of elm wood on which to cultivate their crops and graze their animals. The wood they felled would have provided them with stakes to build stockades to protect their breeding animals from predators like the wolf, lynx and fox. Excavation of these early sites has shown that, as well as seeds and animals, they brought pottery vessels which could be used both for storage and for cooking. Recent research suggests that they coexisted peacefully with the earlier inhabitants of the island. Contemporary sites of both groups, identified by artifacts, are found close to each other so it is likely that the indigenous population traded fish and game for flint implements.

The new farmers built wooden houses which had hearths and pits for storage of their seed grain. They used polished stone axes to fell trees, to fashion wood for building, and, when mounted as a mattock, for cultivation of the soil. The archaeological evidence of agriculture is slight and the abundance of cattle-bones on the dwelling sites suggests an emphasis on grazing rather than cereal cultivation. Nor have we any stones from this early period which might have been used as querns for grinding grains. Cattle will feed eagerly on the shoots of regenerated bushes and trees, so perhaps the woodland clearances were designed to provide such grazing rather than ground for tillage. We have evidence of other animals too: sheep, goats, a domesticated pig, and wild animals like boar, wild birds and, occasionally, even seal and bear.

Over a period of something more than a thousand years, these early farmers developed a remarkable society. The most visible mark the neolithic peoples left on the landscape were their megalithic tombs. These developed as three distinct types. Court-graves were the earliest and we have identified over 300 of these lying mostly to the north of the central lowlands. There are about 300 passage-graves found mainly on hilltops in eastern Ireland. Finally, the crowning achievement of this early society is the great series of tombs in the fertile valley of the River Boyne at Knowth, Dowth and Newgrange. These vast structures, which pre-date the Egyptian pyramids, are unquestionably the work of an advanced and highly organised society. Experts have estimated that as many as four thousand people may have been needed to farm the valley in order to provide the people to build these great monuments and the food to feed them.

Such relatively large-scale farming had a dramatic effect on the landscape. These neolithic farmers used shallow cultivation methods which quickly exhausted the soil. When the land became exhausted they moved on, clearing more woodland. Their old sites, allowed to lie fallow, regenerated themselves over about three hundred years, allowing the farmers to return there.

But they moved on for other reasons as well. It was around this time that the climate deteriorated, becoming colder and wetter, and much of the old woodlands were gradually engulfed by bogs. There had been an earlier period, just after the great Ice Age, when the dumping of glacial deposits had resulted in the flooding of lowland areas. This had resulted in the raising of the great midland bogs and the blanket-bogs of the coastal hill regions. But in this second period the bogs crept inexorably outward and upward, swallowing up much of the ancient woodlands, covering many of the settlements of the first farmers, covering even the summits of the highest mountains.

Today, much of Ireland is still covered by bogs which grew at this time. They are a source of turf for fuel (in Ireland peat is always known as turf) and, as it is cut and stripped away, many strange sights are revealed: the stumps of ancient woodlands, *toghers* (bog roads) made from felled trees and brushwood, the stone-walled field-systems of these early farmers. The bogs conceal, and periodically yield up, many fascinating and invaluable secrets of our early history.

About four thousand years ago another wave of settlers brought Ireland into the Bronze Age. The Beaker Folk were named after their elaborate decorated pots which were found in their burial places—gallery-graves—along with bronze axes and jewellery. These relics mark their owners off from the earlier settlers of the island. A necklace found on the body of a young boy incorporated beads which came from Scandinavia, England and the Mediterranean lands, demonstrating the trading connections these people had with other lands. It is inevitable that such connections introduced a whole new range of plants and animals into Ireland. Metallurgy meant that a far wider range of implements could be made and resulted in the introduction of new farming techniques.

It was these Bronze-Age prospectors, roaming the country in search of metal-bearing rock formations, who first built *fuluchta fiadh*—the ancient cooking sites which are found scattered over the countryside and which endured as a cooking technique into medieval times. A sunken trough lined with stones or wood was built near water. These troughs vary greatly in size but one made out of a recycled, hollowed-out canoe would have held up to 215 gallons of water. A fire was lit nearby and large stones were heated in it. The hot stones were thrown into the water in the trough and quickly brought it to the boil. Large joints of meat were wrapped in straw and put into the water. Recent experiments have shown that it cooked in 20 minutes to the pound weight—the standard modern cooking time! The stones which sometimes split when they were thrown into the water were thrown in a pile on the far side of the cooking site. Many of these ancient cooking-places were discovered because of the characteristic horseshoe-shaped mounds made by the stones beneath the surface. Such sites are widespread. In Co. Cork alone there are over two thousand. At Craganowen in Co. Limerick and at the Heritage Park in Wexford you can see working demonstrations of these *fuluchta fiadh*.

Roughly twenty-seven hundred years ago, in the late Bronze Age, there was a burst of farming activity promoted by the development of farm implements. Around this time too, probably a little later, another group of settlers arrived in Ireland bringing further innovation. Swords and shields replaced the customary hunting spear and they brought with them massive cauldrons, wheeled carts, musical instruments and the ard plough.

This wooden plough must have seemed a miraculous implement at the time because its deeper penetration of the soil meant that land which was exhausted could bear crops once more. But it was susceptible to damage from buried stones which had to be unearthed and removed. The labour of this tended to fix farmers to one place, quickly exhausting the newly enriched soils once more. A rising population living on less fertile lands seems to have caused unrest in the land for the first time. Certainly it is during this period that the first defensive dwelling sites appear—*crannog* lake-dwellings and hill-forts. These settlements and the appearance of distinctive bronze artifacts are the first signs of Celtic intruders on the island. It is tempting to speculate that a race of warlike Celts plundered the island bringing about the collapse of an organised society but there is little real evidence of this. But there is evidence, from recent sophisticated pollen-counting techniques, that this period ushered in a dark age for farming, caused by soil exhaustion, which was to last for about six hundred years.

About 2250 years ago the soils became increasingly unproductive, tillage farming declined again, and an era of semi-nomadic pastoral farming re-emerged. It was during this period that the Irish developed their great passion for *Bánbhianna*—white meats, as they were known to later invaders of the island—a varied range of milk products.

Although the coming of the iron plough would allow the re-establishment of tillage in some areas because of its ability to rip up the top layer of the acid heathlands to reveal the richer subsoils, our only evidence for this is a few early plough-shares found near *crannogs*. These sites are thought to have been permanent dwellings where kings, or at least clan leaders, lived. But, by and large, for many centuries, great herds of cattle reigned supreme. Cattle-raiding was a national pastime. A person's worth was reckoned in cattle which were used as units of value. A man or woman of six heifers, or of three milch cows, became a commonplace. The great pagan religious festivals, their myths and their ritual, all centre round cattle.

Samhain, the autumn festival which began on the 31st October, marked the end of the grazing season when the herds were brought together. Only those beasts fit for breeding were spared from slaughter. The whole extended family or *tuath* assembled and feasted for days on end. *Bealtaine*, the May feast, marked the time when the herds could once again be driven out to open grazing. Two great bonfires were lit and the cattle driven between them to protect them against disease. These great rites were supervised by the druids of the tribe.

Despite its semi-nomadic, pastoral nature, this was a highly developed and organised society in its enlightened and highly structured code of law, its art, its great oral traditions in literature and genealogy. For the ordinary Irish, this cattle-culture was to survive the coming of Christianity, the Normans, Cromwell and his devastations, right up to the threshold of the 18th century.

The *bánbhianna* fascinated strangers to Ireland and there are many written accounts of the Irish predilection for these white meats. As late as 1690 one Englishman wrote: "The people generally are the greatest lovers of milk I ever saw which they eat and drink about twenty several sorts of ways and what is strangest love it best when sourest." Many writers, even as late as this, explain how the various white meats were made and it is usually possible to relate these descriptions to the old Gaelic word for the food. The early Christians have left written record of their own rules regarding to white foods, usually in relation to their fasting, but also describing the food of the ordinary people. Although the sagas and the Brehon Laws were only written down around AD800 they were the written expression of the ancient lore and laws of a much earlier period and contain much that is valuable to us in reconstructing the ancient, pagan way of life before the arrival of Christianity.

Just as the very earliest hunters and gatherers had different summer and winter foods, white meats were divided into these two types. From May until the end of October the milch cows grazing the summer pasture provided abundant milk. No doubt some was drunk fresh, just as it is today, but it was at this time that the Irish passion for soured milk came into its own.

Bainne clabair was a "thick" milk either soured naturally or prepared by putting fresh milk into a vessel which had previously contained sour milk which then soured the fresh. In some cases this would separate out into a kind of liquid cottage cheese.

Treabhantar was a different mixture of fresh milk and buttermilk or *bláthach*, the liquid left after butter-making, which was a drink in its own right. It seems to have been this buttermilk which they liked most, just as country people do today. All of these different methods of souring milk seem to have been ways of increasing the supply of buttermilk which they got in only limited quantities from the making of butter.

Grutha were curds of various types. The Brehon Laws refer to them as a condiment for bread, as summer food for men on sick maintenance, as being paid as rents, and even as fines for the trespass of dogs. They became a normal part of the monastic diet and were a valued food since an army of warriors in 942 were refreshed on their homecoming with "three-score vats of curds which banished the hungry look from the army." They were chiefly a summer food when the cows were in full milk.

Cáis is now the common Irish-language word for cheese of all types but it seems to have referred originally to one specific type. *Fáiscre grotha* was a pressed curd. An attempt was made on the life of St. Patrick by putting poison into some of this cheese. Clearly, it failed! *Tanach* was a hard cheese. Just how hard may be gathered from the fact that Furbaide, the nephew of Queen Maeve, used a piece of *tanach*, which he happened to be eating, instead of a stone in his sling when he killed her. He was as good a shot as the biblical King David, who killed Goliath, because he caught her right between the eyes.

The Vision of MacConglinne, a 13th century poem in Irish, has many varied descriptions of foodstuffs. The hero, sailing in a coracle boat made of beef dripping, passes "strands of dry cheese." The poem refers to "sleek pillars of ripe cheese" holding up the roof of a building he enters. So *tanach* must have been very hard and very dry. The poem also describes *maethal* as a "smooth, sweet, soft cheese" but it was made in a large size because another writer, referring to a person of formidable girth, says "his buttocks were like half a *maethal*."

Grús was a soft curd cheese made from soured buttermilk which was kneaded but not pressed. *Millsén* was a semi-liquid curd cheese made from whole milk set with rennet. *Mulchán* was another hard cheese and one of the last to die out, probably because it was exported in large quantities. It was being made in Waterford right up to 1824 when an English writer, anglicising the name to Mullahawn, says that it was "a cheese made from skimmed milk . . . but of such a hard substance that it required a hatchet to cut it." Whey, the bye-product of cheese-making, was valued as the drink *meadhg*. When it was mixed with water to be drunk on fasting days it was known as *meadhguisce* and skimmed-milk whey was *liommeadghuisce*.

Butter was the greatest symbol of plenty in this society. Made fresh in summer, *imúr* was highly prized. Heavily salted and sometimes flavoured with garlic or leeks, *im* could be stored in wicker baskets and buried in the bog to provide a "high taste" for Lent. It must have been a high, old acquired taste because, if huge amounts of salt with garlic or leeks weren't sufficient, immersion in the bog would have added its own high flavour. Such baskets of bog-butter, buried in ancient times, have actually been discovered. Not, I fear, in an edible condition.

If we add to these fifteen varieties of *bánbhianna* those others which we know they made from the milk from their sheep and goats, then we have reached the "twenty several" of our 17th-century traveller. The dominance in the Irish diet of these white meats can be guessed at by looking at the written reports of the wars waged by successive English generals against the native Irish. These seem to have been conducted as much against their cattle as against the Irish themselves.

In Munster in 1580 we read that "great preys of cattle were taken from the Irish and so has brought them to the verge of famine." In Ulster in 1600, the Lord Deputy "forced all the cows from the plains into the woods so that for the want of grass they would starve and O'Neill's people would starve for the want of milk." Having broken up and scattered the great herds, the English turned their minds to changing the Irish way of life which so irritated them. The English thought the able-bodied Irish men should have more to do than "follow a few cows grazing . . . driving their cattle continually with them and feeding only on their milk and white meats." The sting comes at the end when we see the Englishman's purpose. " . . . if they [the Irish] were exhausted by working in the fields and gardens they would have less energy for raiding." Enough said!

Milk

The Vision of MacConglinne refers to "a delectable drink of very thick milk, of milk not too thick, of milk of long thickness, of milk of medium thickness, of yellow bubbling milk the swallowing of which needed chewing." References to milk of varying thickness abound in early writings and continued until a few generations ago. There were several which were commonly consumed and their consistency was arrived at in different ways. "Clabber" was the collective name given to these beverages by the English and is used of a thick, sour milk which has not yet separated into curds and whey. The process of souring milk to this point is called clabbering. A souring agent like rennet or the juice of plants like butterwort or sorrel was sometimes used.

Thick Milk or Bonnyclabber

In the days before milk was separated from the cream mechanically it was set in large, wide earthenware containers before the fire. The cream rose to the top and was skimmed off. The residue was often soured into a sort of jelly which was taken as a tasty drink, variously known in Irish as thick milk *(bainne clabair)*.

Troander

Not a dish one could make easily today. It resembles the English syllabub or the Scottish Hatted Kit. It is made by taking a measure of sour milk to your cow and then milking the animal directly into the serving cup. It forms a frothy drink which pleased at least one visitor to Ireland in 1699: "I was surprised at the pleasing taste and extraordinary coldness of it." There is a later recipe using whole milk which can be drunk hot or left until it is cold and set to a thick consistency.

White Stirabout (*Leite Bhán*)

  2 cups fresh whole milk
  1 tsp flour
  ¼ tsp grated nutmeg or cinnamon
  1 dssrtsp sugar

Leite, nowadays, is the Irish for porridge but it was used originally for a thick milk gruel rather like the Scottish "brose". Heat the fresh milk to just below boiling-point. Have ready the flour, nutmeg or cinnamon, and the sugar mixed together in a tablespoon or two of cold milk. Stir these into the hot milk. I used to be served this at night as a child on my way up to bed. I remember quite liking it. A much more traditionally Irish milk pudding recipe would be a blancmange made with whole fresh milk and carrageen moss.

Carrageen Blancmange

  1 cup dried carrageen moss
  3 cups whole fresh milk
  1 tbsp sugar

Work the carrageen with your fingers under running water until it becomes pliable. Place the milk, carrageen and sugar together in a pan and simmer them over a medium heat until the carrageen has almost dissolved. Put through a strainer to get rid of any small pieces of seaweed that remain and pour into a jelly mould. Set it to cool in a cool place. Turn it out when it has set and serve it on its own or with any fruit you wish.

Cultured Milk or Yoghurt

While it is true that Ireland did not have a tradition of cultured milk like yoghurt the basic principles behind their thick milks are similar in intention if not identical in taste. What is interesting is the fact that when yoghurt was introduced into Ireland in recent times it became, almost immediately, one of the most popular of the modern manufactured dairy foods. Today you will find an amazing range of yoghurts in our shops made from both cow's and goat's milk and consumed as either a pudding or a thick drink.

Buttermilk

When butter is made the liquid which separates out and drains away from the butter solids is, and always has been, prized above all other milk products in Ireland. Even today, strong, hard-working countrymen (and one famous journalist who is of their number) will wax lyrical on the joys of a draught of buttermilk in the fields. When fresh, buttermilk is foamy, slightly acidic and has almost a fermented quality. It becomes rather sour and flat when stale.

After the introduction of the potato into Ireland, buttermilk became a favourite savour for boiled floury potatoes. This would have been a complete meal for most poor Irish families. Today it is used almost exclusively for making the national loaf—soda bread. Ireland remains one of the few countries where buttermilk can be bought everywhere. Until relatively recent times, and still in some country areas, there are ways of using it which date back to the earliest times.

Buttermilk Drop Scones or Pancakes

> 2¼ cups buttermilk (or sour milk)
> 6 oz fine oatmeal
> 3 oz self-raising flour
> 2 tbsp honey
> 1 tsp baking soda (bicarb.)
> 1 egg
> enough milk to mix a batter

Add the buttermilk to the oatmeal in a bowl, mix them well and leave to soak overnight. Sift together the flour and the baking soda and mix them into the oatmeal batter. Add the honey, the beaten egg and enough milk to make a batter which is slightly thinner than that for ordinary egg pancakes. Heat a heavy pan or griddle over a medium heat and when it is hot place tablespoonfuls of the batter onto it. Leave them until they rise and are covered in bubble holes. Turn and brown on the other side. These are best eaten hot from the pan with butter and honey. I remember being served these as a child in Donegal but they served them with golden syrup and sometimes with whipped cream.

Buttermilk Curds

When milk is coagulated by acids, natural souring, rennet, or crushed herbs, the solids, containing casein and fats, are known as curds and the liquid as whey. In 1698, an Englishman called Dunton described how his breakfast curds were prepared by his Irish host. "The next morning a greate pott full of new milk was sett over the fire, and when it was hott they poured it into a pail full of buttermilk which made a mighty dish of tough curds in the middle of which they placed a pound weight of butter."

The following recipe is more to modern taste and can be used in any of the ways in which you would serve a cottage cheese.

Buttermilk Cheese

>   5 cups buttermilk (40 fl oz)
>   ½ cup fresh cream
>   1 tsp salt

Put all the buttermilk into a large pan and warm to 60°C (140°F) over a low heat. (You will need to use a suitable cooking thermometer.) Keep it at this heat for 15 minutes stirring continuously. Now remove it from the heat and allow it to cool to 32°C (90°F). When it has cooled place a strainer over a bowl and line it with cheesecloth. Pour the contents of the pan into the cheesecloth and leave it to strain. This will take from 6 to 8 hours and you should gently tighten the cloth round the curds as they settle onto the cloth and the whey passes through to the bowl. When all the whey has strained through turn the curds into another bowl and add the salt and the cream. Stir to mix thoroughly. Use butterpats or two broad-bladed knives to shape the cheese on a plate. It is ready to eat at once.

Buttermilk Cheese and Strawberries

>   2¼ cups fresh milk
>   1½ tbsp buttermilk
>   ¼ tsp rennet
>   2 tbsp fresh cream
>   1 lb fresh strawberries
>   sugar

Mix together the milk, buttermilk and rennet in a large bowl and leave to stand in a warm place until solid. Drain off the liquid through a cheesecloth as in the previous recipe. It will take 8 to 10 hours, or leave it overnight. Turn the solids into another bowl and mix in the cream and a little sugar. Set 4 strawberries aside for decoration and thinly slice the remainder. In a serving dish layer the cheese and the strawberries, sprinkling each layer of berries with a little sugar if that is to your taste. Top with a layer of cheese. Decorate with the 4 whole strawberries.

Buttermilk Cream Curd or Quark-Type Cheese

2½ cups fresh milk
5 cups buttermilk

Put the buttermilk into a large bowl. Scald the fresh milk in a saucepan by heating it to just below boiling-point. Add it to the buttermilk in the bowl. Do this quickly and stir the mixture. Allow this mixture to stand until it is cool. Drain the mixture through cheesecloth. Squeeze the curds in the cloth, lightly, from time to time as they are draining. The curds formed will look, and taste, rather like the modern quark-type cheeses: light, creamy, ready to be used as a spread when mixed with fresh herbs, served with fruit, or used as a dressing for baked potatoes. It could also be substituted for the buttermilk cheese in the previous recipe.

Curds and Whey

Little Miss Muffet sat on a tuffet,
Eating her curds and whey.

Miss Muffet, for the purposes of this book being a rather refined young lady, probably of Anglo-Irish extraction, was more likely to have been eating *junket*—a scented, sweetened, spiced pudding originally brought to Ireland by the Normans, in which case, the spider which frightened her away was probably a dispossessed Irishman lurking in the woods near the Muffet family tower-house. Curds and Whey or Junket can

42

be as plain or as sophisticated as you like; I have seen recipes which demand brandy, walnuts, rosewater and exotic spices. But if you mix a half-teaspoon of ground cinnamon, or mixed spice, or 1 teaspoon of caraway seeds into some of the curds from the previous recipe, sweeten this with some sugar to taste and serve it in a small dessert bowl with 5 tablespoons of the whey, also sweetened with sugar, poured over it just before serving, you will have a tasty pudding. The whey from these recipes can also be used in place of buttermilk in the brown bread and scone recipes.

Cream

Irish people today eat far less butter than they did even in the recent past but they still consume large quantities of fresh cream in cakes, desserts and puddings. Oddly enough, there is a puritanical streak in the people that often considers it extravagant to use cream in savoury dishes.

Many of the older people like to have cream in their tea instead of milk, but virtually everyone will confess to an addiction to fresh fruit with cream, either whipped or plain poured. Even today two main fruit-gathering festivals are still celebrated in Ireland. County Wexford in the sunny southeastern corner of the island is the great soft-fruit-growing area and to coincide with the first early crop of strawberries the people of Enniscorthy host the Wexford Strawberry Festival. Lakes of cream are devoured.

Recently, in County Wicklow, just to the south of Dublin, the annual Fraughan Sunday festival has been revived. Whortleberries (*fraochán*) are plentiful where the land has lost nutrients and degenerated into heathlands covered in heather. The bushes are low-sized, hugging the ground in patches, and their dark-blue, juicy fruits grow singly and take a lot of picking. On Fraughan Sunday whole families head for the foothills of the Wicklow Mountains to pick the berries from a patch that they have probably been watching for weeks on their Sunday afternoon jaunts. The berries are usually eaten with fresh whipped cream or used as a pie-filling. Clothes and children are stained deep purple for days afterwards.

Cheese

No doubt the discovery of cheese was an accident of curd-making, the result of leaving the soured milk too long with a natural souring agent, thus precipitating much harder, tougher curds. But there is clear evidence that cheese was also a staple food early in Irish history and that some of the cheeses were "hard".

It seems reasonable to speculate that milk, curds and butter became the summer food of the people, while the hard cheese, which would keep better, would be kept for the autumn and winter. We have no evidence as to the degree of pressing such cheeses received but in the *Book of Lismore* a youth is described as carrying three of them on his back, suggesting that they were readily transportable. It has been speculated that since *grutha* means curds then the words *fáiscre grotha*, which is the name given to one of these early cheeses, could well mean "pressed" curds.

Cheese of one kind or another formed a substantial part of the Irish diet right down to the close of the 17th century. During the 18th century its consumption progressively declined and the making of it was practised less and less. By the early 19th century agricultural writers of the time can state that "Cheese is not an article of Irish produce; it is brought to the tables of the affluent as an indulgence." To the present day, cheese remains an alien item to many Irish country people.

When I was a child in the nineteen-fifties the only Irish cheese commonly eaten was a revolting "processed" cheese which came in small triangles wrapped in silver paper and smelled of boiled milk. It could never have inspired anyone to become fond of cheese. However, in the last fifteen years, slowly at first, there has been a revival of farm cheese-making in the country. A few, resolute souls who were not, in the main, farmers but city folk moved to the country, determined to be self-sufficient in lonely farmhouses, growing their own vegetables and milking the odd cow, goat or sheep. Then, just as in ancient times, they needed to find a way to preserve their surplus milk.

Supplies were so scarce at first that people "in the know" whispered their source to friends, almost afraid to mention the revival of this ancient craft. Today there are many good Irish farmhouse cheeses being made. There is a very creditable farmhouse blue cheese, *Cashel Blue*, and, it has to be admitted, other cheeses which are of less consistent quality. But the best, like *Milleens,* made by one of the pioneers, Veronica Steele (and her husband), in West Cork, can stand comparison with the very best cheeses made anywhere. Irish farmhouse cheeses are worth seeking out in any good delicatessen and no self-respecting Irish restaurant should be without its selection of local cheeses.

Even the large co-operative creameries, for so long content to contribute to the European butter-mountain, now have large cheese factories. Most of their produce can only be classified as a so-called cheddar "type" which is exported in vast quantities to the United Kingdom. But there are notable exceptions. Mitchelstown Co-op. produce an excellent hard *grana* cheese called *Regato* which is much in demand in Italy and Greece and makes a very acceptable and much cheaper substitute for *Parmesan*. There are several brands of *feta* cheese which are excellent, and acceptable Dutch Edam-types. Let the experimentation continue.

CHAPTER THREE
GRAINS, VEGETABLES AND FRUITS

Seventeen hundred years ago as the island began to emerge slowly from the historical darkness of the Iron Age there was an upsurge of agricultural activity and a corresponding increase in population. It seems likely that all the land capable of cultivation was being worked and the Irish began to emigrate to Scotland, to Wales, to Cornwall and to the Isle of Man.

About fifteen hundred years ago the Christian religion reached Ireland. A monastic organisation, governed by the abbots of monastic foundations, rather than a diocesan organisation administered by bishops, was a characteristic of early Irish Christianity. The monastic settlements were to have, ultimately, an important influence on the farming methods and foodstuffs of the people.

At this period a typical homestead was a circular construction of earthen banks, known as a *rath* or *lios*, or one of stone walls, known as a *cashel*. These circular enclosures vary in diameter between 20 metres and 125 metres. The larger ones might have up to three outer banks, were possibly the homesteads of clan chieftains, and are often referred to as *dúns* or *cahers*. There are over forty thousand of these dwelling places identifiable today and their wide distribution is clearly seen in the placenames of towns and villages in modern Ireland: Rathmullen, Lisdoonvarna, Cashel, Dunmore, Caherciveen. Some of these sites remained in use until as late as the 17th century.

Within the enclosure there would have been wooden huts where the family unit lived, small farm buildings and an open green space where livestock could be penned in time of emergency. The serfs, slaves and prisoners of war probably lived in huts propped against the inside of the bank or in the outer ditches. The density of these sites suggests that they were designed to be visible from one to the other within the clan's area of influence. In a countryside where cattle-raiding was endemic, this would have been an important defensive consideration. The smaller sites, worked by independent farmers, had about 70 acres of good land attached to them. This holding, reckoned to be the value of two healthy *female cumal* or, slaves, would have been backed up by woodland, where the farmer had the right to cut timber, bogland, where he could harvest turf, and pasturage for his livestock's summer grazing. The equivalent of today's "strong" farmer lived much the same sort of life but had roughly ten times the amount of farmland, as much as 700 acres. Neither of them owned their land in the way that we understand it today.

Land was the property of the *derbhfhine*, all those descended from the same great-grandfather. Each member of the king's *derbhfhine* was eligible to succeed to the throne, if elected by the freemen of the *tuath* or tribe. Each king of the *tuath* was bound by personal loyalty to a superior king who might, in turn, be subject to a provincial king. The lower king showed his loyalty to his overlord by giving him hostages, accepting a stipend from him and rendering a tribute of animals, white foods, grains, malt and herbs. The right to hold land did not pass down by primogeniture or to a chosen heir but was portioned out to the immediate kin, thus causing complicated subdivision of holdings.

Monastic enclosures, too, varied greatly in size but the larger, more important ones formed, much later, the beginnings of the first urban settlements in Ireland. Monks and lay people lived side by side within these settlements. The deliberately spartan monastic diet, with its emphasis on grains and vegetables rather than meat and white foods, led to a wider development of arable farming and vegetable growing.

Corn of several sorts was grown: oats, barley, wheat and a little rye. Of these, wheat and barley had been in cultivation since neolithic times but oats were introduced during this period. Although soft wheats can be successfully grown in the

48

wet climate of Ireland, oats and barley are much better suited to our conditions.

Oats gradually became the principal grain crop and oaten bread the common bread of the people. It remained so in large areas of rural Ireland right down to the 19th century when those preparing for the long voyages of forced emigration baked flat, dry oat cakes to sustain them during their time on the ships. Barley bread was associated with the spartan diet of the monks. Their rules tell us exactly how much they were allowed to eat at different times of the year. Barley was also used for making beer. Wheaten bread was always regarded as the greatest delicacy—the bread of feast-days and the tribute of chieftains and kings. In much later times, amongst the poor, a bread made from pea and bean meal was common and, during and after the great potato famines of the 19th century, a bread made from maize flour was often resorted to.

In many parts of the country a loaf of bread is called a cake. This often caused me great disappointment as a child, when I'd be offered a cut of cake, and then find myself presented with a piece of fresh griddle or soda bread instead of a creamy sponge cake. The latter would have been referred to as a sweet cake. This usage is a direct throwback to the old Scandinavian word for a flattish round of bread made from any grains, which could be either leavened or unleavened, and was known as a kake or *kaak*. It survives today, outside Ireland, in Scottish oat cakes which were once a staple bread of both countries.

In the larger monasteries and, later, in the Norman castles and houses, bread was baked in ovens. But until quite recent times the ordinary people cooked and baked at the open hearth on a *lec* (bakestone) or a *lan* (flat griddle) above a bed of embers. They made flattish cakes of leavened bread about one inch thick. Before cooking it would be scored or cut into four pointers or farls (a term still used today in Ulster) and would be eaten, with butter, while still warm. Leavened bread was also baked in a pot-oven or bastible, a deep, flat-bottomed pot with a close-fitting lid on which glowing embers of turf were piled to give even cooking heat.

In early Christian times bread was leavened with barm, a brewing agent, which was later made from potatoes. A mixture of bicarbonate of soda and buttermilk came to be used, in more recent times, to produce the much-loved Irish soda bread or brown cake. This fine bread is still enjoyed today by the native Irish and tourists alike. Bread was always eaten fresh, served with a condiment of butter. As the old Irish phrase has it: *"Nua gacha bídh agus sean gacha dighe!"* — food should always be eaten as fresh as possible and drink well-matured. Outside the monasteries, relatively little bread was eaten; as late as 1533 the King's Council in Ireland comments that the Irishry "can live hardily without bread or other good victuals." But a great deal of grain was eaten in the form of various types of porridge, still a traditional breakfast food in Ireland today.

Like milk, the Irish served porridge in various thicknesses, made it from a variety of grains and flavoured it in several different ways. This was surely a matter of convenience in a pastoral society, being both quicker and requiring less equipment to prepare than bread. *Brothchán* was the old Irish word for porridge, which in modern Irish is called *leite*. In recent times porridge has come to mean oat porridge. The grains were boiled in water, in sheep's or cow's milk, and flavoured with butter, salt, cream or honey.

In the Brehon Laws, which persisted as rules for conduct of the Irish outside of the English-governed area of The Pale until the late 16th century, it states:

> "The children of the inferior grade are fed to a bare sufficiency on stirabout made of oatmeal on buttermilk or water, and it is taken with stale butter. The sons of chieftain grades are fed to satiety on stirabout made of barley meal upon new milk taken with fresh butter. The sons of kings are fed upon stirabout made of wheaten meal upon new milk taken with honey."

The thinnest porridge was an oatmeal water, *brothchán* or *meanadhach* reminiscent of today's refreshing barley water. A later version of this, much-beloved of travelling pedlars, was porter *meala* which they made by pouring a measure of porter (stout or ale) over some dried meal which they always carried with them. This was allowed to stand for a while before it was drunk. *Sowans* was a mildly fermented drink made from either the inner husks of oats or unsifted, milled grains mixed with water and allowed to stand until natural fermentation produced a rather sour drink. Stirabout was a thicker mixture, a porridge as we know it, made by trickling the grains into water which is kept stirred to prevent lumps forming. The grains were husked and split and known as pinhead oats. It takes about half an hour to cook.

The porridge leftovers could be used to make *leite faoi chupóig*. The cold thick porridge was cut into slices and wrapped in vegetable leaves, either cabbage or dock, and baked directly on turf embers. *Práibín* was made by coarsely grinding mixed grains which had been first toasted and browned in a dry pot over the fire. Served with milk or cream, and honey or salt, it resembled a modern-day muesli.

Vegetables, as far as the pastoral farmers were concerned, were predominantly wild roots and leaves and would remain so for many centuries to come. Later invaders often comment upon the "curious salads" eaten by the native Irish. Watercress (biolar) and sorrel *(samhadh)* and shamrock were eaten and a root *imus,* which is thought to have been a type of celery or parsley, as well as charlock *(praiseach),* a wild member of the cabbage family. But the vegetables most prized and most frequently mentioned in the Brehon Laws were the strong vegetables like leeks *(foltchép)*, onions *(cainneann)* and garlic *(creamh)*.

The traditional way of growing vegetable crops was in raised beds or ridges, called lazy beds. Developed by the first farmers forty-five hyndred years ago, the method has nothing at all to do with being lazy and a lot to do with being clever. It is a sophisticated way of coaxing the best out of thin wet soils by careful management, and a method widely used, especially in the west of Ireland, right up to the end of the 19th century, and even later by some diehard traditionalists.

Today it is possible to see the pattern of these beds under the surface of the ground stretching right up the sides of mountains to heights much higher than are cultivated today. The remains of these ridges are easier to see than the ruins of the abandoned cottages to which they were attached. Using only a spade to fold back on themselves, towards a central line, two cuts of the topsoil, a thicker, dryer ridge is created with drainage trenches running down each side. The shape of the bed could be adjusted to suit the needs of individual crops at various stages of their growth. The fertility of the raised bed and the texture of its soil could be improved by the regular addition of manure, sand and seaweed. When a bed had been cropped regularly for a period it was divided down the central ridge and the soils thrown outwards over a layer of manure and seaweed to form two new beds drained by a central channel.

The crab apple and the bramble were both native fruits and had been eaten since the first settlers reached Ireland. The monks established orchards and the earliest manuscripts differentiate between the wild and the cultivated apple. The Brehon Laws name the apple as a fruit of the chieftain class and speak of it in glowing language: "fragrant in smell, delicious in taste, and delectable in colour," and the monks were very protective of their orchards. St. Comgall is said to have blessed a garden from which thieves were stealing the apple trees of his brethren and the culprits were struck blind. Their annals record the harvest of each year and monastic rules specify regulations governing the amounts the monks were allowed to eat: "If they be large, five or six of them with bread are sufficient; but if they be small, twelve of them are sufficient." Kings, it seems, ate rather more. A chieftain who had to entertain King Cathal MacFinguine had, amongst other things, to provide a bushel of apples to take the edge off his insatiable appetite. In pre-Norman times the apple appears to have been the only cultivated tree and orchards were an integral part of post-Norman manors and settlements.

The monastic settlements were often the most secure buildings in an area and in times of unrest, valuables of all kinds, including stocks of food, were brought to them for safe-keeping. The monastic lands were endowed by clan chieftains and the abbot of a monastery was often a member of that chieftain's family. The coming of Christianity did not herald the end of cattle-raiding or faction fighting between rival tribes. Monasteries were raided in exactly the same way as any other farmstead belonging to a tribe and food, livestock, treasures and people were carried off by the victors. When the raiders were another Irish tribe, the despoiled *tuath* had, in theory at least, recourse to the law. The threat of judicial sanctions involving loss of status or honour (both very important in ancient Irish society), like the exclusion from ritual sacrifices, were sometimes sufficient to control an offender for a time.

Not surprisingly, the Vikings were not inhibited by such threats and were not amenable to the authority of Irish kings or laws. These fierce raiders had begun to threaten Ireland, just as they brought terror to much of the rest of northern Europe, from the 8th century on. But their raids on the monasteries, although never as numerous as those of the Irish themselves, brought out the wrath of the monks far more. From the 7th century to the 16th century the burning and pillaging of churches was mainly the work of the native Irish themselves. It was a destructive habit which began before the Norsemen came and lasted long after they were absorbed and forgotten. The annals of one monastery record quite clearly that in a 25-year period (AD795-820) the monastery suffered 112 raids. Only 25 of these were perpetrated by Vikings and 87 by the Irish themselves.

It is possible that the Vikings were more violent in their attacks than the Irish. After long sea-voyages, with relatively small numbers of men, they would be anxious to replenish their food stocks and seize precious objects and slaves, with which to trade, as quickly as possible before the local tribes could gather against them. Where better to do this than the well-peopled and well stocked and provisioned monasteries?

The Vikings, who quickly established bases *(longphorts)* along the eastern and southern coasts of Ireland from Strangford Lough down to Dublin, at Wexford, Waterford, Cork and Limerick, had a great impact on the everyday life of the country. They were traders, who plied the seas from Russia to the Mediterranean and were responsible for the introduction of many new foods into the country. They exported slaves, metalwork, wool, hides and skins from Ireland and imported plums and other fruits, walnuts, wines, olive oil, herbs and spices into the country as well as amber, jet, ivory, silver, lead, glass, and pottery. Their initial settlements grew in size and developed into the first real urban settlements in the country as the Vikings became absorbed into the island's population. Dublin (Dyflin or *Dubh Linn*, Black Pool) was an immensely important Viking stronghold, as one commentator puts it: "filled with the wealth of barbarians." The Scandinavian sagas also testify to its importance, often urging their pro-tagonists to "fare south" to Dublin for "that is the route most famous" and "many are in the habit of making this Dublin voyage." The Vikings of Dublin paid a levy to the Irish king Brian Boru of 150 vats of wine a year and another com-mentator wrote of the abundance of wine in Ireland, which was paid for by "the return to Poitou of hides of animals and skins of wild beasts."

Oats

Always a most important grain in Ireland, oats are a nutritious, health-promoting food and deserve to be widely eaten still. Today there are many different types of oats to suit a range of recipes.

When oats are brushed, polished and then cut into three pieces, they are called pinhead oatmeal. Until recent times this was the meal used in Ireland to make breakfast porridge and is still used for soups and broths and for grinding to make the finer textured flours needed for baking. Coarse ground oatmeal can be used to make porridge, to make oat cakes and for coating meat and fish prior to frying or grilling. It can also be used in stuffings. Medium ground oatmeal is used for milk puddings and as a thickening agent in soups and stews. Fine ground oatmeal, sometimes called oat flour, is a good baby food and can be used in bread, cakes and pastry.

The bran or outer skin of the oats and the inner germ (growing point) of the grains are often separated from the oats during processing and sold separately, the bran as a source of added fibre, and the germ as a vitamin and mineral supplement to be added to other foods.

Oatflakes, porridge oats, rolled oats and flaked oats are all, more or less, the same thing. The oats are softened by steam and flattened by rollers during a process which partially cooks the oats allowing them to cook fully more quickly than pinhead oatmeal. These are the most commonly used oats for making porridge in Irish homes today.

Porridge

In Ireland today porridge is usually made on water, seasoned with salt, and served hot for breakfast with cream or milk, and sugar or honey. Although traditionally made from whole oats or pinhead oats, it is now made from oatflakes which are sold as quick-cook porridge oats. I certainly consider it, and so does my Scottish husband, the best of all breakfast foods. You will read of all kinds of things, from raisins to curry spices, which can be added to it, but they are spurned by the majority of Irish and Scots who like it well-salted during cooking (essential to the taste) and served with cream and sugar or honey.

For each serving you will need 1 ounce (3 tablespoons) of oatflakes and a cup of water. Some people use a half-and-half mixture of water and milk and you should add a good big pinch of salt during cooking. Bring the oatflakes to the boil in the liquid, add the salt and stir constantly while it is cooking. When it begins to thicken and bubble, turn down the heat and let it plooter away for 5 to 6 minutes. If it seems too thick for your taste add a little more liquid. Stir it occasionally to prevent it sticking to the pan. No doubt this is where the word stirabout came from. To make larger quantities just multiply the ingredients by the number of servings you need.

Sloke and Oatmeal Cakes

  1 cup cooked sloke
  6 oz medium oatmeal
  bacon fat

Chop the cooked sloke (seaweed) finely and add it to the oatmeal. Mix them together thoroughly. Form them into cakes about 2 inches (5 cm) across. Heat the bacon fat in a frying pan and when it is hot (but not burning) fry the cakes in it until browned and crisp on both sides. Serve for breakfast with bacon and eggs.

White Breakfast Pudding

Modern white puddings are a pork product with an amount of added cereal and spices. In less affluent times they were an oaten pudding, flavoured with whatever fat was to hand and herbs. I had experimented several times with meatless puddings but found them insipid and bland. Jack Hick, pork butcher, friend, and prize-winning pudding-maker, forced to sample some of my efforts, came up with this combination which is true to the oaten pudding but has enough taste to please a modern palate.

  4 oz grated pork flead or beef suet
  6 oz coarsely ground oatmeal
  1 tbsp wholemeal flour
  2 oz pork liver
  ½ stick of celery
  1 small onion peeled and finely chopped
  ½ cup broth (from the liver)
  ½ tsp salt
  ½ tsp pepper
  1 tbsp dried thyme

Firm the liver in half a cup of boiling water for about 3 minutes. Drain it and reserve the liquid. Grate the liver finely. Pour the liver water over the oatmeal and soak for a few hours or overnight. Grate the pork flead or beef suet. The flead is the fine inner membrane of pure pork lard which surrounds the pig's stomach. Soften the onions and the finely chopped celery in a small amount of the fat. Now add the rest of the suet, the onions and celery, the thyme, salt and pepper, to the soaked oatmeal. Mix thoroughly. Shape into a long sausage about 1½ inches in diameter. Roll the sausage up into a cloth and tie both ends with string. Bring a large pot of water to the boil and place the pudding into it. Turn down the heat and simmer it for about 1 hour. Take it out and let it cool before removing the cloth. It can be eaten hot or cold, or cut into slices and fried in bacon fat to accompany a traditional Irish fried breakfast. An older serving would have been to roast the whole pudding, basted with bacon fat, to be served with an apple or onion sauce. Fresh thyme can give the pudding a greenish tinge and old dried thyme can give a musty taste. I compromised by quick-drying freshly picked thyme in the microwave oven.

Oat-bread

I must own up to having had trouble producing a reasonable oat bread until my friend and fellow cookery-writer Honor Moore came to my rescue. Honor is a Co. Down woman, trained in Home Economics in Belfast, who has been writing knowledgeably and well about food for "more years than she cares to remember." She has been a tower of strength and encouragement to me during the writing of this book, particularly with recipes from the northern half of the country, because, apart from the fact that she is herself a superb and adventurous cook, she actually knows what a great many of these traditional recipes should taste like, since many of them remained in common use up there long after they had disappeared from tables in the south.

½ lb fine oatmeal
½ lb strong white flour
   (or use a mixture of white flour and wholemeal)
3 cups buttermilk
1 tsp bicarbonate of soda
1 tsp salt
2 tbsp honey (or brown sugar)

Put the oatmeal into a large bowl. Warm the honey, add it to the buttermilk and pour the mixture over the oatmeal. Leave it to stand overnight in a cool place. When you have pre-heated your oven and are ready to bake the bread, add the salt and the bicarbonate of soda to the flour and sift this over the soaked oatmeal. Mix them together well to get a fairly stiff dough. (You may need to add a little more buttermilk at this stage.) Divide the mixture into two, well-greased, one-pound (500g) loaf tins. Bake for 45-55 minutes at 200°C (400°F, Gas Mark 6). They are cooked when they sound hollow when removed from the tins and tapped on their bases. If you like a hard crust allow them to cool on a wire rack. For a softer crust, wrap them in a clean cloth to cool.

Oat Cakes

The early oat cakes were made simply of oatmeal and water but the addition of a proportion of wheat flour and fat makes a cake that is easier to handle while baking and rather tastier to eat.

½ lb medium oatmeal
1 oz white flour
⅛ cup boiling water
2 tbsp melted bacon fat or butter
a good pinch of bicarbonate of soda
a good pinch of salt

Mix the flour and the oatmeal together in a bowl. Place the boiling water in a measuring jug and mix in the fat. Add the salt and bicarbonate of soda to the water and tip it over the oatmeal and flour mixture. Mix quickly and knead lightly into a ball. The dough should be firm but not dry. The exact amount of water depends on the absorbency of the flours. Sprinkle a pastry board with more oatmeal and press the dough into a flattish circle. Roll out lightly and quickly into a thin cake about 7-9 inches in diameter. Slide this onto a flat baking tin or pie plate and trim the edges to make them neat. Should the dough split as you roll it out just press it back together again with your fingers. Cut into 8 farls or pointers. Bake at 180°C (350°F, Gas Mark 4) for about 45 minutes. The cakes should be lightly tinged with brown. Store in an airtight tin. Delicious with cheese.

Oat and Wheat Biscuits

4 oz fine wholemeal flour
4 oz oatflakes
4 oz butter or margarine
4 oz sugar
1 beaten egg
½ tsp salt
½ tsp baking powder

Cream the butter or margarine with the sugar in a bowl until it is light and fluffy. Add in the dry ingredients and then the egg. Mix well. Clean hands work best with this mixture. Turn the mixture out onto a surface floured with wholemeal flour and knead it. Divide it into two equal pieces and roll out one of them until it is about a quarter-inch thick. Using a 2-inch (5 cm) biscuit cutter cut out the biscuit shapes and place them on a greased baking sheet. Incorporate the offcuts into the second piece of biscuit dough. Keep rolling out and cutting until you have used up all the dough. Bake the biscuits (in batches if necessary) at 200°C (400°F, Gas Mark 6) on the middle shelf of the oven for about 15 minutes. They should be golden brown. Watch them carefully towards the end of this cooking time because they can catch very easily and burn quickly. The full amount of sugar gives a fairly sweet biscuit and it can be reduced if you do not have a particularly sweet tooth.

Wheat Bread

Irish-grown wheat is what is known as soft (like our weather) and the hard wheat needed to make white yeast breads is imported. However, traditional Irish wholemeal bread is made from homegrown flour because the leavening process does not rely upon the interaction of yeast with gluten during kneading.

The Irish still make and eat a very distinctive wheat bread of ancient lineage in their homes today. Even those (including many men) who have no interest in *fancy* baking will regularly bake a brown cake. A cynic might maintain that it is the poor quality of most commercially made breads which has kept the traditional loaf alive but, over and over again, visitors to this country rave about the homemade brown bread they are served for breakfast, and at tea-time, everywhere from farm guest-house to five-star hotel. Another reason for its stubborn survival is that it is a simple bread to make, quick and, once you have the hang of it, very easy to master. In fact, the less you do to it, the better the bread.

Two of the oldest foods in Ireland, wheat flour and butter-milk, are leavened with bicarbonate of soda (often referred to as bread soda in many cookery books) which is the traditional leavening for most Irish breads and scones. The soda, when mixed with certain acids in the buttermilk and with its moisture, acts as the raising agent. Its action can be limited by the production of other chemicals during the process so it is essential to make and to bake the bread quickly. The flour can be wholemeal or white. It is often made using a mixture of the two and the proportions vary according to the taste of the person making the bread. Stoneground, wholemeal flour is readily available all over the country and extra wheat or oat bran (occasionally wheat or oat germ as well) is often added to raise the fibre content and enrich the bread.

Brown Soda Bread (Cake)

18 oz flour
1 tsp bicarbonate of soda
1 tsp salt
2 cups buttermilk, sour milk or whey

Use a half-and-half mixture of white and wholemeal flour. Mix this with the salt and the bicarbonate of soda in a wide bowl. Make a well in the centre and pour in about half of the buttermilk. Using a round-bladed knife quickly draw the flour into the liquid. Keep adding liquid until almost all the flour has been gathered into a sloppy dough. Gently and quickly knead in the last of the flour in the bowl. You want to end up with a soft dough but may not need all of the liquid depending on the flour. Turn the dough out onto a floured board and quickly shape it and knead it into a circle without cracks which is about an 1½ inches (3-5 cms) thick.

Do not be tempted to knead the bread in the manner you would knead yeast bread. It is not necessary. The whole process from the moment you add the buttermilk to the ingredients in the bowl should take no more than 3 minutes. Any longer and the action of the bicarbonate of soda is lost.

Bake on a floured baking sheet or a floured cast-iron pot at 200°C (425°F, Gas Mark 6) for 35-40 minutes. It should be lightly browned and sound hollow when tapped on the bottom with your knuckles. Turn out onto a rack to cool. This is the basic traditional recipe.

Griddle Bread (White Soda Bread)

In our house this is known as Dinky's Bread in honour of a dear friend who was joint mother to our son. When he was born I was an actress in a weekly television drama series. I had little choice but to go back to work one week after he was born. Dinky (Anna) Heffernan, now sadly dead, was a fine actress herself, from an old theatrical family, who had travelled the halls of rural Ireland "fitting-up" night after night. She had raised three fine sons herself and she stepped into the breach when my son was born. She became his "second" mother. When I arrived back from work to collect him I would be greeted by a happy, smiling child and, invariably, a loaf of fresh griddle bread to take with me. I can smell it yet. She cooked it every day of her life. It shows how great the love of fresh homemade bread is in Ireland if you think of the terrible difficulties she must have had to do so while "on the road." She cooked it on top of an old-fashioned paraffin stove because she said its gentle heat made the best bread. The stove was kept solely for this purpose long after the need for it as a heater had passed. It remains my son's favourite bread, to be eaten for breakfast with grilled smoked rashers from the inimitable Jack Hick of Sallynoggin.

Follow the instructions in the previous recipe for brown soda bread but use only plain white flour. It is only the cooking method which is different. Heat the griddle or a large flat pan over a medium heat. Roll out the dough, quickly and gently, into a circle about 1½ inches thick. Score it into 4 pointers or farls. You can separate them or leave them touching. As soon as you put the bread onto the griddle turn the heat down to very low and allow the bread to cook for 5 minutes. It will rise and form a light dry skin on the upper surface. Turn the heat up again (not too much) and cook until it is lightly browned underneath. Turn the bread over and cook at the same heat on the other side. The whole operation will take from 30 to 40 minutes depending on the heat under the griddle.

Some people like to eat their griddle bread hot, with lashings of butter; some allow it to cool on a wire rack, others wrap it in a clean cloth to cool and this gives it a softer crust. Leftovers can be fried for breakfast in bacon fat. Split the farls down the centre and fry them until crisp and golden brown.

Curranty Cake

There are probably as many recipes for this favourite tea-time treat as there are home-bakers in Ireland. This version is called "Nan's Curranty Cake." The television serial I worked on for sixteen years was filmed on location in deepest County Meath. The traditional breakfast on film sets is hot bacon-and-egg baps (small bread rolls). But on our set we got hunks of hot brown soda bread and this curranty cake baked in huge cakes about 2 feet wide. You had to arrive at the canteen early to get your share of curranty cake. Still hot, packed full of plump fruit, spread thick with fresh butter and washed down with strong tea milked with creamy, unpasteurised milk straight from the cow. Wonderful! This is a smaller-scale recipe which Nan herself gave me.

1½ lb plain white flour
4 oz currants
4 oz sultanas
1 tsp bicarbonate of soda
1 tsp cream of tartar
2 cups (roughly) buttermilk
2 tbsp butter

Sift the dry ingredients together into a wide bowl and rub in the chopped softened butter with the tips of your fingers. Add the fruit, mix through, then add the buttermilk. The method and cooking instructions are exactly the same as for soda bread. This is best eaten the day it is cooked with lots of butter. Leftovers are delicious toasted or used to make bread and butter pudding.

Buttermilk Scones

> 12 oz plain white flour
> 2 tbsp butter
> 1 tbsp sugar
> 1¼ cups buttermilk or soured milk
> 1 level tsp bicarbonate of soda
> 3 tbsp sultanas

These scones are really just a variation on the recipe for curranty bread and you can use a mixture (to your taste) of wholemeal and white flours. Follow the instructions for curranty cake to make the dough but roll out the dough until it is a good inch thick (2.5 cm). Use a 2-inch (5 cm) biscuit cutter to divide the dough into scones. Bake on a floured baking sheet at 200°C (425°F, Gas Mark 6-7) for about 15 minutes until the scones are well risen and lightly browned. Serve while still warm with butter and a good jam or preserve. Crab apple jelly is particularly good.

Treacle Bread and Scones

A commonly met variation on the buttermilk scone recipe is the addition of treacle to the mixture. To ensure that the treacle mixes evenly through the dough put 1 tablespoon of treacle into 2 tablespoons of fresh milk and warm them together. Stir the melted treacle into the milk and decrease the amount of buttermilk in the recipe.

Brack

Brack is the traditional bread of Hallowe'en (All Hallows Eve, 31st October). This is the eve of All Saints' Day (1st November) in the Christian calendar but the ancient Irish pre-Christian festival of *Samhain* was celebrated over several days com-mencing on this day.

Two main types of brack are made in Ireland, barmbrack, which is a yeast-leavened bread cake, and a tea-brack raised with baking powder. While it is traditionally eaten at Hallowe'en, when a ring is often inserted into the cake to herald marriage before Easter for the girl who discovers it in her slice, brack is a popular tea-time cake throughout the year. Brack is always eaten buttered in Ireland. This recipe, a tea-brack, is very dark, rich, moist and fruity and will keep well, over several days, in a tin.

Tea-brack

5 oz plain white flour
5 oz dark cane sugar
5 oz raisins
5 oz sultanas
1 tbsp mixed peel (optional)
1 tsp mixed spice
1 cup black tea
1 tsp baking powder
1 egg (beaten)

Weigh out the fruit and cane sugar. Place them in a bowl and pour hot, unmilked tea over them. Stir well to dissolve the sugar and allow this mixture to stand overnight. The fruit will emerge wonderfully plump and moist. Stir it well before use to make sure all the sugar is dissolved. Sift the flour, baking powder and the ground mixed spice into a wide bowl. Beat the egg. Mix, alternately, some of the egg and some of the flour mixture into the fruit until all the ingredients are thoroughly mixed together. Turn out the mixture into a well-greased 7-inch (18 cm) cake tin which has been lined on the bottom with greaseproof paper. This makes it easier to turn out the brack when it is cooked. Bake at 160°C (325°F, Gas Mark 3) for about 1 hour.

This brack is usually given a sticky, glazed top which is brushed onto the brack in the oven about 10 minutes before the end of the cooking time. I use warm honey but a sugar syrup works just as well. Remove the cooked brack from the oven and allow it to cool for about 10 minutes before turning it out of the tin. In an airtight tin this brack will keep without drying out for 4 or 5 days.

Buttermilk for Bread Making

The characteristic taste and texture of traditional Irish breads and scones is largely due to the use of buttermilk, or soured milk, as the liquid. Now, while fresh milk can sometimes be substituted, that indefinable character will be lost. It is possible to make an acceptable buttermilk substitute at home if you have the time and the patience and cannot live without that wonderful Irish bread.

If you do substitute fresh milk then you should use baking powder (a commercial mixture of bicarbonate of soda and cream of tartar) instead of bicarbonate of soda. You can successfully sour fresh milk by adding 2 teaspoons of lemon juice to each cup of milk and allowing it to curdle for half an hour.

Buttermilk Plant

This is not unlike the principle behind making yoghurt at home and it makes a perfectly acceptable buttermilk substitute. With care the culture will live indefinitely and it is a good idea to get some of your friends to start their own plants because, if left unattended for too long, your plant can up and die on you. You can start again with a culture from one of your friends. It sounds much more complicated than it is in practice. In the old days in Ireland this was known as winter buttermilk.

    1 tbsp sugar
    1 tbsp dried yeast
    2½ cups fresh milk
    ½ cup boiling water

Cream the yeast in 2 tablespoons of warm water in a cup or bowl. When the yeast has reactivated and formed a healthy head of froth add it to the mixture of milk and boiling water. Tip the whole lot into a wide-necked jar with a screw-top lid. The jar should be large enough to hold at least 5 cups of liquid. Place the jar in a dark, warm place and leave it for 3 to 6 days. Give it a gentle shake each day.

After about 5 days it should be ready to use. Place a colander over a bowl. Line the colander with scalded butter muslin and strain the contents of the jar through this. The liquid which passes through to the bowl is used for baking (or drinking) and the curds which remain in the muslin are washed in warm water (to remove the last traces of buttermilk) and then used to start your next culture.

Spoon the washed curds back into the jar. This, and the spoon, must have been thoroughly scalded in boiling water. Mix 2½ cups of fresh milk with a half-cup of boiling water. Add these to the jar with the curds. Replace the lid and place the jar in its warm, dark place. You should do this every 5 days whether or not you have a use for the buttermilk.

Kerry Apple Cake

I've never been given a convincing reason why this cake is called a Kerry Apple Cake as the recipe is common all over the country.

    3 large cooking apples (peeled, cored)
    8 oz white flour
    3 oz butter
    3 oz caster sugar
    1 tsp baking powder
    1 large egg (beaten)
    good pinch grated nutmeg
        (or ground cinnamon or ground cloves)
    demerara sugar to dust cake
    a good pinch of salt

Peel, core and finely chop the apples. Sift the flour into a bowl and work in the butter with your fingers. Mix the sugar, salt and baking powder together in a small bowl then stir this into the flour and butter mixture. Add the finely chopped apples and use the beaten egg to mix everything into a soft dough. Line a greased 8-inch (20 cm) cake tin with greaseproof paper and turn out the dough into this. Cover the top of the cake with brown sugar mixed with the ground spice. Bake for 45 minutes at 180°C (350°F, Gas Mark 4). Test with a skewer, which should come out clean from the centre of the cake, before removing the cake from the oven. This cake is traditionally eaten hot from the oven, but it is possible, if it is freshly made, to eat it cold.

Porter Cake

This is another of those classic Irish cakes which everyone's granny makes to her own unique recipe. This version was given to me by Paula Daly who has probably taught more Irishwomen to cook than anyone else through her radio programmes, her demonstrations and her splendid series of McDonnell's Good Food Cook Books.

    6 oz wholemeal flour
    6 oz plain flour
    1 rounded tsp mixed spice
    1 level tsp baking powder
    8 oz dark brown sugar
    8 oz butter or margarine
    3 large eggs (beaten)
    ½ cup Guinness
    6 oz raisins
    6 oz sultanas
    3 oz walnuts (roughly chopped)
    grated rind of 1 orange

Place the wholemeal flour in a mixing bowl and sieve the plain flour, mixed spice and baking powder on top. Mix thoroughly.

Cream the butter or margarine with the sugar until light and fluffy. Beat the eggs into this a little at a time, beating well between each addition, adding a little of the flour mixture if the batter curdles. Fold in the flour, a little at a time, along with some of the Guinness. When all the flour and Guinness are added, fold in the fruit, nuts and orange rind. Fill the mixture into a prepared tin lined with greaseproof paper. Smooth the top. Bake in a pre-heated oven at 150°C (300°F, Gas Mark 2) on a low shelf for 3¼-3½ hours.

Hallowe'en Pudding

This delicious pudding comes from the area of Lower Ards in Ulster. It is a much less elaborate, lighter pudding than the traditional Christmas pudding which it resembles. We serve it at Christmas too.

4 oz brown breadcrumbs
2 oz plain white flour
2 oz sugar
½ tsp bicarbonate of soda
1 tsp mixed spice
½ tsp salt
3 oz butter
½ lb (250 gm) mixed dried fruit
1 tbsp treacle
¾ cup buttermilk

Rub the butter into the flour with your fingers and then add all the other ingredients so that they are mixed through, using just enough of the buttermilk to give a soft, but not sloppy, mixture. Place the mixture into a well-greased pudding bowl large enough to allow for expansion. Cover the bowl with a double thickness of greased, greaseproof paper held tightly in place with string. Steam the pudding for 3 hours. Serve with whipped fresh cream.

Vegetables

It would be flying in the face of the facts to maintain that the Irish had, or have, a great tradition of vegetable cookery. Vegetables have always been an important part of the Irish diet but the limited range of varieties which thrive in our climate, usually strongly flavoured ones like leeks, onions, carrots, parsnips, cabbage, globe artichokes, turnips and beets, has not inspired native cooks down the ages. Vegetables are often just boiled and served, dressed with some variation on the theme of a white sauce. In our defence it should be said that many of our soups and stews depend on a high content of vegetables but this has encouraged many of our cooks, until relatively recent times, into cooking vegetables for too long—often to the verge of disintegration. Too many Irish restaurants, particularly those at the lower end of the market, still serve overcooked vegetables. But times do change and there is a growing realisation that it is not necessary to "boil the bejasus" out of them.

Leek and Oatmeal Soup

This leek and oatmeal soup is a master recipe for several other soups using different vegetables. For those of you who are more used to using flour or puréed vegetables to thicken a soup, oats may seem a strange substitute. But I beg you not to be unadventurous. Not only is the recipe a simple one but the soup's distinctive flavour may come as a pleasant surprise. This is a favourite in our household.

> 5 cups milk or good meat stock
> 2 oz flaked oatmeal
> 3 cups sliced leeks (white and green)
> 2 tsp melted lard
> 2 tbsp fresh chopped parsley
> a good pinch of ground mace
> salt and freshly ground black pepper

Wash and clean the leeks thoroughly before slicing them up very finely. Heat the fat in a pot and add the flaked oatmeal. Stir the oatmeal over a low heat until it begins to brown slightly and smell toasted. Add the milk or the stock and season. Add the finely shredded leeks and simmer gently for 45 minutes. Stir in the chopped parsley just before serving.

Nettle Soup

A delicious variation made in spring when the nettle-tops are young. This soup is particularly good when made with turkey stock. Just substitute 3 cups of nettle-tops and three chopped scallions (spring onions) for the leeks in the previous recipe. You can also replace the oatflakes with a cup of diced potatoes.

Kale Soup

Substitute 3 cups of finely shredded kale leaves for the leeks. Even the stems of young kale can be very tough but if you are sure that the kale is young the stems can be shredded or grated. You might need to give it a little longer cooking than for the leeks or nettles. It is possible to use this method to make a cabbage soup as well, using some of the water in which a bacon hock was cooked. In order to stop the cabbage overcooking do not add it until the oats and the stock have simmered together for half the cooking time. This will be very salty unless the bacon was soaked overnight with several changes of water before cooking. Watercress is another variation you might try but a good meat or vegetable stock should be used rather than bacon water.

Bacon, Pea and Barley Soup

This is what is known in Ireland as an *atin' and drinkin'* soup. If the truth were told we are not, as a people, all that fond of drinkin' soups, much preferring a good thick meal in a bowl. A tale is told of a country farmer who went to an *atin'* house in a certain town on a fair-day. When a bowl of clear consommé was placed before him he looked at it with such patent loathing and suspicion that the waitress asked him if there was anything wrong with his soup. "Let them," he said, "what ate the meat, drink its water!"

    1 bacon hock
    6 oz pearl or pot barley
    1 cup dried split peas
    1 small head of green cabbage
    2-3 leeks
    2-3 carrots
    2-3 celery stalks
    ¼ swede
    2 potatoes (peeled, diced)
    parsley
    thyme
    bay leaf
    freshly ground black pepper

The hock is the pig's rear foot up to the elbow and can weigh well over a pound. If cooked until really falling off the bone it has a surprising amount of succulent meat and makes a wonderfully gelatinous broth. It should be soaked overnight in several changes of cold water and can often be improved by boiling for 5 minutes in another change of water before being added to the soup. The peas and the barley should be soaked in about 2 pints of water for 2 or 3 hours.

Place the peas and barley with their water into a large pot along with the hock. Add enough extra water just to cover the hock completely. Add the herbs and the pepper. Bring it to the boil then reduce the heat and simmer, covered, until the meat is completely tender. This might take 2 hours, sometimes less. Peel, chop and dice all the vegetables except the cabbage. When the meat is cooked, remove the hock onto a plate and add the chopped vegetables to the pot. Simmer them until tender. (About 30 minutes.) Remove the meat from the bones and break it up into pieces. The skin and fat are considered a delicacy in Ireland but you might not feel inclined to eat them. Keep the meat warm or return it to the soup along with the cabbage. About 15 minutes before you mean to serve the soup either cut the heart of the cabbage into quarters or shred it very finely. Add it to the soup in the pot and cook for just 15 minutes. Serve this soup with hunks of fresh wholemeal soda bread. Definitely a meal in itself.

There are many variants of this soup, some adding lentils, others using the water in which mutton or beef has been cooked, but this is the preferred one in our house.

Onions

Onions have a central place in many Irish dishes as an essential flavouring but have long been valued as a vegetable in their own right. Few Irishmen could contemplate eating a beefsteak without a dish of fried onions on the side. Dean Swift who had strong views about food had his own theories about removing the odour of onions.

> *There is in every cook's opinion*
> *No savoury dish without an onion.*
> *But lest your kissing should be spoiled*
> *The onion must be thoroughly boiled.*

I must admit that I myself can do without onions boiled but my husband, who is a Scotsman, would happily make a meal of onions, boiled, fried, baked, or any other way. He maintains, like many before him down the centuries, that nothing contributes to the health of mankind more than onions and garlic (which he consumes in vast quantities). As he remains astonishingly healthy, despite heavy smoking, alcoholic indulgence, a punishing (if sedentary) workload, little sleep, and no exercise but an odd weekend trout-fishing, he may have a point.

Baked Onions

Choose firm medium-sized onions and remove the root and the loose outer skins. Simply put them in a baking tin and bake them at 180°C (350°F, Gas Mark 4) for about 1½-2 hours. Serve with salt, butter and lots of chopped fresh parsley.

Onions in Milk

Onions are often served like this in the north of Ireland. Peel the onions carefully making sure that you leave the root intact. Split each onion about halfway down into quarters. Into the cuts put a spoonful of butter mixed with chopped fresh herbs (thyme, sage or parsley) and salt and freshly ground black pepper. Place the onions into a pan just large enough to hold them upright and add sufficient milk to come about a third of the way up the bulbs. Bring quickly to the boil then turn down the heat to low, cover tightly, and barely simmer them, for at least 40 minutes to an hour, until they are tender. Serve in a soup plate with the cooking milk and fresh bread or floury boiled potatoes.

Cabbage

This is the most commonly committed murder in Ireland. It was the habit in the country to cook the cabbage along with the bacon. Fine so far, you might think, but it depends at what point you add the cabbage. You can imagine the state of the cabbage if it goes in at the beginning with a bacon joint which might require several hours cooking. This would still not be uncommon. You have been warned. A less sulphurous flavour is achieved using the following method.

    1 large head of fresh green cabbage
    1-2 cups bacon water, diluted if very salty
    1 tbsp butter (or bacon fat)

Shred the cabbage finely, removing the thicker parts of the stalks. Depending on the amount of cabbage you have, take some water in which a bacon joint has been cooked. If you have soaked the bacon before cooking this should not be too salty. Bring this water to a rolling boil in a large enamelled or stainless steel pot. Add the cabbage to the boiling water and cook for 3-5 minutes. The length of time depends entirely upon the variety of cabbage. Young, fresh, spring or summer cabbage cooks extremely quickly. Savoy or the dark, crinkly-leaved winter cabbage takes considerably longer to become tender. When cooked strain the cabbage thoroughly and toss quickly in butter or stir fry it quickly in the bacon fat.

A delicious and distinctive additional flavour can be achieved if you stir fry the cooked cabbage in a little olive oil in which one garlic clove, puréed with 4 dried juniper berries and a little salt, has been fried for half a minute before the cabbage is added.

Seakale

Known as strand cabbage in Co. Donegal (hence its Irish name *praiseach thrá*), seakale grows wild round much of the Irish coast on sandy and shingle beaches. It puts out its first leaves in March and traditionally, once you had located your source, sand and pebbles were drawn up round the plant as it grew, to cover it completely and blanch the shoots. After two to three weeks, always provided you could find it again, it was uncovered. The stems would have blanched and only a few small leaves would remain at the top of the stems. The stems were eaten. Now it is possible to buy cultivated varieties and a most delicious vegetable it is.

If you pick wild kale then wash it thoroughly to remove sand and grit. If you have the cultivated variety you will need to remove the earth from the stem. Tie the stems into little bundles large enough to serve each individual. Simmer it in a covered pot for about 20 minutes. Serve with melted butter and lemon juice.

Samphire

There are still coasts where you can gather samphire, the Carlingford Peninsula in particular. It is an umbelliferous plant with thick fleshy leaves and a very strong, pungent smell and taste. It is boiled until tender in water, drained and then served tossed in butter. It can sometimes be obtained pickled.

Mushrooms

Mushrooms grow widely in Ireland but they are getting rarer and a good source is unlikely to be divulged except to one's nearest and dearest. We gather field mushrooms, boletus, the occasional beefsteak fungus and shaggy inkcaps each year. Our source for chanterelles has dried up lately. Oyster mushrooms are now being grown commercially in the country and ordinary cultivated mushrooms are a thriving business here. Field mushrooms are the only wild fungus eaten by most Irish people today and they are at their best just fried in a little butter or bacon fat or cooked in cream.

Mushrooms in Cream

> 1 lb field mushrooms
> 2 tbsp melted butter
> 1 cup fresh cream
> fresh thyme or parsley
> salt and freshly ground black pepper

Wash but do not peel the mushrooms. Place them in a single layer in a buttered baking dish and dribble the butter over them. Bake in a pre-heated oven at 200°C (400°F, Gas Mark 6) for a few minutes until they soften. Pour over the cream and heat the cream through in the oven but do not allow it to boil. Sprinkle with the chopped fresh herbs and the salt and pepper just before serving. Serve with good bread to mop up the juices. These are a good accompaniment for grilled meats.

Strange Irish Salad

> *"the cresses on the water and the sorrels are at hand"*
> (Translated from the Irish by Sir Samuel Ferguson)

We can only guess at the strange green leaves and herbs that went into the strange salads which are often mentioned in the old accounts of the Irish way of life. Sorrels, shamrocks and cresses are frequently mentioned, but there are a myriad of

77

other edible green leaves and flowers growing wild in the Irish countryside. If you know what you are picking then choose three or four, or more, from the following list: sorrel leaves, watercress, dandelion leaves, beech leaves, hawthorn leaves, beetroot leaves, comfrey, chickweed, nasturtium leaves and flowers, elderflowers, clover flowers, wild mint, wild thyme, wild garlic, lamb's lettuce, chive leaves and flowers, borage leaves and flowers. Wash them and dry them gently. Just before serving toss in a vinaigrette dressing made from good olive oil and a cider vinegar.

CHAPTER FOUR
MEAT AND GAME

As the Viking settlements along the eastern seaboard of Ireland grew in wealth and importance during the 10th and 11th centuries it was inevitable that the attention of the Norman invaders of the neighbouring island would be drawn across the Irish Sea. The Normans arrived in Ireland, lest the more nationalistic among us be tempted to forget, at the invitation of an Irishman. It is usual to lay the whole blame for subsequent history at the feet of Dermot McMurrough who "brought the foreigner in." But that is to be unfair to the man and to ignore the facts of Irish life in these centuries.

The Irish tribes were in a state of almost constant internecine strife, being a quarrelsome, litigious race (as they remain to this day), who did not subscribe to the notion of one kingdom, one king. Despite the best efforts of a whole series of minor provincial kings to proclaim themselves *Ard Rí* (High King) they only managed to reign, as a contemporary source has it, "with opposition." With around 150 petty kingdoms in the country the possibilities for strife were endless and were increased when the Vikings, who seemed to enjoy a fight as much as the native Irish, wove a shifting web of alliances with different tribes. When the Normans invaded England in 1066 they found a similar situation among the Anglo-Saxons.

When the Normans came to this country in 1169 they found it a much harder proposition to conquer than England and never fully succeeded in subjugating its people. In time they began to intermarry with the Irish and eventually became, in the timeworn phrase, "more Irish than the Irish." Four hundred years after the Normans came, the great Irish families were still there to be counted. But the Normans did have a marked effect on Irish life, particularly in relation to the ownership of land and its agricultural use.

The changes in the ownership of land in Ireland in the period between the coming of the Normans and the present is complex, involving dispossession, successive "plantations" of settlers from England and Scotland and bitter, often brutal, religious and political discrimination. This was rooted in the constant determination of successive English dynasties to prevent Ireland being used by their enemies as a back door into the larger island.

The Tudors were completely frustrated by the lackadaisical efforts of the Normans at colonisation. By that time the Norman hold on the island had shrunk to the relatively small area of The Pale, an area largely confined to the east and south of the country. The Tudors were not convinced that the "old English" had the means or the will to defend Ireland from attack, but their own efforts at colonisation were, ultimately, hardly more successful. The Stewarts managed to subjugate parts of Ulster through the plantation of Scots farmers but it took the harsh, puritanical army of Oliver Cromwell to force the Irish into retreat and exile. By 1660 most of the lands of Ireland had changed hands. Previous landowners, both native Irish and "old" English (the latter more likely to be referred to now as the "rebel" English) were banished by Cromwell "to Hell, or to Connaught" in the far west of the island.

It is a popular misconception that Cromwell slaughtered vast numbers of the Irish, yet this is hardly borne out by the facts. There were atrocities and executions but the numbers involved were relatively small and few of these were the common people. Even men who had borne arms against Cromwell were allowed to emigrate to Europe and over 30,000 of them did so. The English were more interested in the wealth of the country. Those "native" landowners who had taken part in the rebellion had their lands confiscated; those who had not were allowed to hold land to the amount of their previous holdings but in Clare and Connaught. The rest of the country became the property of the government and was, in the main, used to pay off its creditors—officers and soldiers who had served

Cromwell without proper payment, and adventurers and suppliers who had funded and ordnanced the government army. Most of these new landowners managed to hold on to their newly acquired properties even after the Restoration of the monarchy in England under Charles II. Thus was the land and wealth of the country consolidated in Protestant hands while the old Irish way of life retreated into the western fastnesses of the island.

In contrast to their failure to effect real change in the ownership of land in Ireland, the Normans were to have a profound influence on the way the land was used for agriculture. The pre-Norman Irish were happy to farm at subsistence levels. There was land enough for all if you counted your wealth in cattle. Food was grown to feed the family and agricultural by-products, mainly skins and hides, could be traded for more exotic items like wine, spices and olive oil. But the Normans had come from the European mainland where agriculture was more highly developed, where men counted their wealth in acres of land held and where ploughed land was valued for the ability of its rich soils to grow corn crops for the markets of Europe.

Once farming depends upon cash crops, to use the modern phrase, it is at the mercy of the market in those crops and when the market fails, through wars or fluctuating demand caused by falling population in times of pestilence, farming is in deep trouble. Irish farming, after the Normans, was to get into deep trouble time and time again.

To the Normans, Ireland must have seemed under-populated and under-exploited. Though few in number, the Normans quickly changed agricultural practice in the country and many of the Irish chieftains were happy to change with them because they could recognise the wealth the changes might bring. The Normans settled the richer agricultural lands of the eastern parts of the country in a rough line from Skibbereen in West Cork, north to take in Galway, then up to Coleraine in the far north. Within this continually shifting line they swiftly began to build their fortified farms and to enclose land in a manner never before seen in the country. They introduced the open-field system and three-crop rotation. The feudal system of land-tenure was enforced within the Norman sphere of influence. Irish kings and chieftains were displaced and their lands were granted to tenants who would support the feudal lord. Some of these tenant farmers were foreigners but numbers of the old Irish tenant-farmer class or *biattach* stayed where they were. The day-to-day life of the ordinary people changed little at first. Instead of food tributes to their chieftain they paid food rents to their new master—the lord of the manor. If you were already of the old Irish *unfree class* (a typical Irish euphemism for a slave) you became a feudal serf.

The first centuries of Norman settlement coincided with a rising European population and a period of warmer, drier weather which allowed the cultivation of good crops of wheat, with which to feed this growing market, and the supply of wool from sheep to clothe it. Sheep were important to the Normans who used them to manure the arable land and to supply wool as an exported cash crop, milk to make cheese for winter use and meat to eat. As well as greatly increasing the sheep flock the Normans brought many other animals and plants to Ireland. They brought freshwater fish to breed in ponds, rabbits to breed in great warrens, doves to breed in dovecotes, the common hare to course alongside the native hare, the fallow deer to supplement the dwindling stocks of the native red. They introduced peas and beans, and flax with which to make linen.

The Normans like the Tudors after them were passionately fond of the chase whether it be hawking for game birds, coursing hare, or hunting deer and the wild boar. While the Irish had hunted and trapped for thousands of years there is little evidence to suggest that they saw it as "sport." They hunted for food and to keep down predators. Let us also set aside the myth that the Normans and the Tudors deforested the country. By the time the Normans came to Ireland the Irish woods were largely gone. The evidence of the density of the Iron-Age sites suggests that there was little room left in the country for wildwood. There is some pollen evidence to suggest that the violence and disruption of the Viking and early Norman periods actually allowed some new woodland to appear on deserted farmland, but for a thousand years Ireland appears to have had less woodland than England. By 1600 it has been estimated that "forested areas" accounted for one-eighth of the land but it seems likely that as little as 3 per cent of the country was still "wooded."

The Irish have always taken whatever they fancied from any outside cultural influence and the modern Irishman's firm belief that a dinner is not a dinner at all but only an excuse for one if it does not contain a *"plate of mate,"* would appear to date back to the Norman period. If the weather had stayed dry beyond the Middle Ages, the history of Ireland might have been very different. But it became wetter and colder, making good wheat hard to grow. The Black Death decimated the population of continental Europe, Britain and the Irish urban centres. By the time of the Tudor plantations there were already two distinct Irelands. The well-kept, farmed lands of The Pale (already much diminished from its early boundaries), and "beyond The Pale," the large areas of un-drained bog, the lakes, mountains, and secondary woods of the mere Irish; land fit only for the old Irish way of farming, of which the Tudors disapproved, called *creaghting*. Here whole communities were constantly on the move, drifting from the protection of one lord to another.

It was not all they disapproved of: "They eat their meat half raw," and rarely accompanied by bread, "they will not kill a cow except it be old and yield no milk." But in times of shortage the Irish "bleed their cattle and mix the blood with grains, milk or butter." Here is the origin of one of Ireland's truly great dishes—drisheen or black pudding (*drisín* or *putóg dhubh*).

When times were not quite so hard they would have a great feasting, remembering no doubt the ancient ways of killing off at *Samhain* all except the milch cows. A Tudor commentator writes that when they do kill a cow "they distribute to all to be devoured at the same time." This old custom of sharing with guests and neighbours the very best of what you have survived even the harshest times in Irish Ireland. Even in later times when they were struggling to survive on their tiny plots of land in the West, with often only a single pig to provide the meat for a year, they would still send choice morsels of fresh pork—the liver, the pork fillet steak, the puddings and brawns—to their neighbours. Stephen Gwynn described the divisions made in 1600: the head, tongue and feet to the "smith, the neck to the butcher (the man who killed the beast), 2 small ribs (that go with the hind-quarters) to the tailor, the kidneys to the physician, the udder to the harper, the liver to the carpenter and the sweetbreads to her that is with child." Strong farmers, when they had beef, sent joints to neighbours, particularly at Christmas and other festivals. Always, it seems, when the Irish did eat meat, they wanted lots of it—Irishmen serving as footmen in great houses in Tudor England would "save their meat up for days, to eat it all at once in one huge helping."

From the managed and cropped woodlands which still existed in the country the Tudors exacted a heavy toll of mature timber. The great oaks whose mast had, for countless centuries, been the rich autumn feed of Irish swine, were ruthlessly felled as a cash crop. Just how important this annual mast harvest was may be seen from this description of the great plain of Macha from the sagas:

". . . and no mast was ever like its mast for size and fragrance. When the wind would blow over it the odour thereof would be smelt throughout Erin, to what point soever the wind would carry the scent, so that it was a heartbreak to the swine of Ireland when it reached them."

The mature oak wood flowed out of the country to build ships and houses, to be made into charcoal and into barrels. As often as not these barrels were filled with heavily salted Irish beef, an ancient Irish delicacy, which was exported in vast quantities to the newly discovered West Indies in exchange for even greater quantities of sugar for the English. In Ireland this favourite dish of exiles (corned beef and cabbage), right down to the present, was eaten on High days as a festive treat. But it was never as common as bacon on the Irish menu.

The pig, whether fresh as pork or salted as bacon, was the favourite food of the native Irish. The earliest sagas, the ancient laws, the monastery rules, even the granting by the Normans to their tenants of rights of pannage (grazing of the woods) for their pigs, attest to the centrality of the pig to the Irish diet. For while cattle and sheep may be kept for other products like milk, butter, hides and wool, the pig provides only meat and it was for meat that it was kept from ancient times.

Every last bit of the pig is used in Irish cooking: the head for cheeses, brawns and the tongue; the trotters for *crúibíns*; the griskins, ribs and kidneys in stews; the blood and other unmentionables to make both black and white puddings—this latter being a peculiarly Irish delicacy. Today the Irish are less adventurous than other countries in the making of sausages but this may not always have been the case. No doubt our damp climate, which is not suitable for the air-drying of sausages, and the Irish passion for bacon, which meant that as much as possible of the carcass was cured, has a lot to do with this. But we know that sausages were made in early Christian times because two intriguing types are referred to in *The Vision of MacConglinne*. *Maróc* and *indrechtán* are intriguing simply because we have no way of knowing what went into them or how they were made. If only one of the monks had been interested in cooking then we might have found out from his marginal doodling.

By the mid-17th century much of Ireland was once again under pasture, the better to rear vast quantities of red meat for export to Britain. At a time (1660-1760) of wretched poverty for the vast majority of the ordinary Irish people the Irish economy was almost totally dependent on the sheep and cattle trade with Britain. But the very success of these exports in the British market threatened the British farmers and resulted in heavy duties being levied on Irish sheep and cattle exports and then a total ban on those exports. Irish wool was also punitively taxed on entry. At a time when the population of Ireland was increasing rapidly, with a perversity frequently apparent in Irish history, the country was poised to become dependent upon the potato as a staple food of the poor, with catastrophic results.

Game

Pigeon

It was the Normans who first systematically bred pigeons for the table, building, often elaborate, dovecotes to house hundreds of birds. But many of the smaller farmsteads in The Pale had smaller ones to hold a dozen or so birds. Elaborate recipes exist for stews and pies but my own experience, living in north County Dublin next to a keen gunman (of the sporting variety), is that in these rather more affluent times only the breast is sliced off the bird and plucked. Today they are most often used as an ingredient in a good terrine or game pie and it is quite common to see two pigeon breasts packed together for sale in the better game shops.

Grouse

It is sad that the native red grouse is such a rarity in Ireland today and that it is virtually impossible to get even introduced birds, apart from the occasional brace, in September. These are usually young birds and you will realistically need one per person. Later, towards Christmas, when they mature you will just get away with a bird between two people.

4 young birds
8 rashers of fat bacon
2 cups of rowan berries
    (fraughans, redcurrants or cranberries will do)
flour
1 cup red wine

Wipe out the cavities of the birds thoroughly and dry the outsides. Place half a cup of the berries into the cavity of each bird. Tie two slices of fat bacon (streaky or belly rashers are best) over the breast of each bird. Roast for 20-30 minutes in a pre-heated oven at 200°C (400°F, Gas Mark 6). The timing depends upon the size of the birds and how well you like them cooked. With 10 minutes cooking time left remove the bacon slices and dust the breasts with seasoned flour. Replace the birds in the oven along with the bacon slices to finish their cooking time. When they are ready place each bird onto a slice of toast or a slice of crisp fried bread and keep them warm while you prepare the gravy. To do this add the wine to the pan juices which will include the juice from the berries along with the bacon fat. Stir this over a high heat for 2-3 minutes to reduce it slightly. Do not thicken it or add any seasoning. Serve with game chips. If you omit the fried bread or toast you could serve the birds with a simple bread sauce and a rowan, fraughan, redcurrant or cranberry jelly is permissible.

Hare

Roast Hare with Sauce Irlandaise

This is a distinctly odd recipe from that doyen of Victorian cookery teachers Mrs. A. B. Marshall. Her cookery book, a massive success at the time, contains only four Irish recipes—perhaps from an Irish cook who had worked in one of the great Irish houses—but although the ingredients and garnishes are typically Irish there is always the possibility that the recipes have no connection with Ireland at all.

1 young hare
½ lb pork larding fat

for the sauce:
1 pint lightly thickened brown sauce (a combination of
    a roux, good beef stock and 1 tbsp chopped tomato)
½ cup port
1 tbsp redcurrant jelly
juice of 1 lemon
½ small onion (chopped fine)
1 bay leaf
sprig of fresh thyme
1 sliced tomato
6 crushed black peppercorns

Cut the larding fat into suitable neat strips and use a larding needle to insert them neatly over the saddle and rump of the cleaned and dried hare. Truss it neatly for roasting. Mrs. Marshall set him, if her illustrations are to be believed, with his legs neatly folded towards the centre of the plate and his ears pointing alertly upwards. Most people today would rather remove the head as it could be difficult to look this handsome animal straight in the eye. Roast in a pre-heated oven for one hour at 180°C (350°F, Gas Mark 4). The good Victorian lady suggests as little as 25 minutes without specifying any temperature. But this seems too little even allowing for their liking the flesh rare and the fierce heat generated by their reflective roasting methods (on a constantly turning spit before an open, red-hot fire).

While the hare is roasting prepare the sauce. Put all the ingredients into a pot and simmer them gently for 10 minutes. Skim off any scum. Mrs. Marshall's disciples would have forced it through a tammy cloth at this point. As this was an invention designed to develop massive muscles and shoulders on already hefty young scullery wenches you may just pass it through a fine strainer or mouli-sieve. Re-heat in a bain-marie and serve hot. The hare should also be accompanied by a salad of water-cress leaves with a vinaigrette dressing.

Rabbit

Rabbits have passed into and out of favour since they were introduced by the Normans. Today they are farmed commercially and young, tender rabbit makes a perfect small roast. The rabbit is still a wild animal however and those you might be presented with by sportsmen can be older and tougher. Then it is perfect for the classic Irish treatment—simmered until tender then finished, browned and crisped, in the oven. Rabbit, stewed with cider or ale and bacon combines a number of Irish flavours to give a tasty winter dish.

Rabbit Stew with Bacon Dumplings

1 rabbit (jointed)
1 onion
2 sticks celery
2 cups ale or cider
1 oz butter

for the dumplings:
4 rashers of rindless streaky bacon
4 oz self-raising flour
1½ tbsp beef suet (grated)
1 tbsp fresh chopped parsley
3 tbsp water

Peel the onion and chop it and the celery very finely. Stew these in the butter until soft. Remove them with a slotted spoon and fry the joints of rabbit (which should be dusted in seasoned flour) in the butter remaining in the pan until they are browned on all sides. Place the rabbit with the onion and celery in a pot. Deglaze the frying pan with some of the ale and add this to the pot with the rest of the ale or cider. Bring this to the boil quickly then cover the pot and reduce the heat. Simmer for about 1 hour until the rabbit is tender.

To make the dumplings, first grill the streaky bacon rashers until they are completely crisp. Chop them up when they are cool into a fine dice. Sift the flour and salt into a bowl and add the grated suet, chopped parsley and the bacon. Mix to a dough with the water. Shape into 8-10 little balls. Add them to the pan with the rabbit stew about 25-30 minutes before the end of cooking. They should be cooked through and well risen. You could make the dumplings with a mixture of flour and cooked, mashed potato in equal quantities.

There is an Italian variation of this rabbit stew which I often cook and which I find utterly delectable. Replace the ale or cider with 2 glasses of dry white wine and instead of the vegetables simply add a good sprig of fresh rosemary. Delicious with good bread to mop up the gravy.

Venison

It should be remembered that bears and lions lived in the prehistoric forests of Britain, though they were probably extinct by the time of the Normans. Of the surviving forest animals William the Conqueror designated red deer, roe deer, the imported fallow deer and wild boar as "beasts of the forest" and reserved their meat for himself. The meat of all four was called venison. Wolves, badgers, foxes, martens, wild cats, otters, hares, rabbits and squirrels were also hunted, but because they were not "beasts of the forest" were not protected. In the unenclosed land outside areas designated as "royal forest," unless the land had been specifically granted as a "warren" to an individual, anyone could hunt these animals. Interestingly, by our terms, the swan was also designated a bird of the forest and therefore the king's exclusive venison.

Eating deer meat was not previously as widespread in Ireland as it became during the Norman period. Bone remnants at prehistoric sites show it to be far less significant than the pig, particularly, and other meats and fish. It remained so for all but the "incomers." Today, farmed "venison" (exclusive insofar as it now means deer meat alone) is beginning to make an impact on the market because it is a lean, and in some minds therefore "healthier," meat and significantly less expensive than beef or lamb. We eat quite a lot of wild venison at home because we have a sporting friend. It can be uncertain of age and can need tenderising and slow cooking. Farmed venison is always killed young and is always tender. Deer meat is so lean that it must always be "larded" to prevent it drying out during roasting or grilling. It is quite usual to marinate even farmed venison for a day or two.

> 2-3 lb haunch of venison
> 6 oz bacon or pork fat
> sheets of flead fat to cover
> 4 oz pork dripping
>
> for the marinade:
> 1 cup wine or cider vinegar
> 2 cups dry white wine
> ½ cup olive oil
> 1 large onion (sliced)
> 2 carrots (sliced)
> 3 large sprigs parsley
> 3 sprigs fresh thyme
> 6 crushed black peppercorns
> 6 crushed juniper berries
> 1 tsp salt

Make sure that your game-dealer removes the outer membrane and draws the sinews from the haunch. Cut the bacon or pork fat into thin strips and use a larding needle to insert it into the haunch. When you are finished the haunch should have the look of a bald, blunt hedgehog. Mix all the ingredients for the marinade in a large bowl and immerse the haunch completely. It needs at least 8-12 hours to marinate and if you are at all doubtful of the beast's age then give it 24-36 hours in a cool place. Turn the joint frequently in the marinade.

When you are ready to cook it remove it from the marinade and dry it completely with kitchen paper. If you can get sheets of flead pork fat then tie these round the joint so that at least the top of the joint is completely wrapped in fat. If you are using dripping, render it down and paint the joint with about half of the fat. Roast in a pre-heated oven on a rack at 180°C (350°F, Gas Mark 4) for 20 minutes to the pound plus 20 minutes over. With regular basting, this should produce a joint which is still on the rare side which is the way venison is served in Ireland. If you prefer it well done then roast it for 30 minutes to the pound plus 20 minutes more. If you have a joint which weighs more than 4 lb then reduce the cooking time to 15 minutes per pound (rare) and no more than 25 minutes per pound (well done).

Seakale is a perfect vegetable accompaniment but celery is also acceptable. Cabbage with juniper berries and garlic is also a favourite vegetable with venison in our household.

Game Sauce

This is a very useful sauce to accompany a number of game dishes.

   1 tbsp finely chopped carrot
   1 tbsp finely chopped onion
   1 tbsp finely chopped celery
   2 tbsp good olive oil
   1 tbsp flour
   2 cups good meat bone stock
   1-2 tbsp rowan or redcurrant jelly

Heat the oil and gently sweat the vegetables in it until they are soft and just beginning to brown at the edges. Add the flour and cook it until it is brown but not burnt. Add the stock to the pan and allow it to simmer for 40 minutes. Keep it well stirred. Skim it, strain it and return the thickened sauce to the pan with the rowan or redcurrant jelly. Stir it over a gentle heat until the jelly has completely integrated.

To serve this sauce with the venison you should thinly slice the meat having first removed the outer fat wrapping. Pour a small amount of the sauce over the sliced meat and serve the rest of the sauce at table. Accompany the meat with what our guests always refer to as "posh fried bread"—croutons of thinly sliced bread fried until golden and crisp in a mixture of butter and good, fruity olive oil. These can be prepared in advance and kept warm in the bottom of the oven between layers of absorbent kitchen paper. I always serve a little dish of the jelly used to flavour the sauce.

Rowan Jelly

In Ireland the rowan tree is called the Mountain Ash. The Celts made wine from its bright scarlet berries and used them to flavour mead. It is a traditional accompaniment to venison and game birds. It used to be necessary to go up into the hills to collect the ripe berries but now you can see them in most suburban streets and gardens. I think I'd still be inclined to gather mine in the countryside as far away from traffic fumes as possible.

> 3 lb ripe red rowan berries
> 2 lb cooking apples (crab if possible)
> 4-5 cups water
> 1-2 lb sugar

Place the berries, the apples (washed but not peeled) into a pot with about 5 cups of water. Bring this to the boil and boil it for about 40 minutes. Strain the contents of the pot overnight through a jelly bag. Measure the juice which passes through into the bowl. You will need 1 lb of sugar for each 2½ cups of juice. Boil the juice in a heavy-bottomed pot for 10 minutes then add the correct amount of warmed sugar. Boil again for about 10 more minutes, skimming off any scum which forms. Test for setting in the usual way and when the setting is right pour the jelly into sterilised jars and seal them at once. This stores almost indefinitely as long as the seal remains intact.

I also make a jelly from ripe elderberries using this method and flavour it with fresh, lightly bruised, thyme leaves.

Pork and Bacon

We have more recipes for the various parts of the pig than for any other animal. It was the food of the poor and of the gentry alike and the recipes range from the simplest of peasant stews to the most wonderful of prime, cured hams. While some pork was eaten fresh, much of it was salted and cured to make it last and often shared, in a "round" with neighbours.

When the pig was slaughtered, it was bled and cleaned and the carcass was split lengthways from tail to snout. Sometimes the head was detached in one piece. The fillets, known in Ireland as pork steaks, were removed and eaten fresh along with the kidneys, heart, liver, brain, sweetbreads, stomach, feet, head and tail. The hams were often treated separately for curing (or roasting in the wealthier establishments). What remained was the *flitch* for bacon curing. It was usually, but not exclusively, dry cured, by rubbing, over a period of time as long as two weeks, with a mixture of salt, sugar and saltpetre. It was then dried and often smoked over a mixture of juniper berries, turf and oak. Today, real, dry-cured bacon is pretty hard to come by. Most of our bacon is now processed in large factories, wet-cured in brine and "smoked" by various chemical means (often producing a result closer to dyeing) the better to make it acceptable to some export market be it in Gt. Britain or Japan.

A few pork butchers survive, working in the traditional way, and when you find one "cleave unto him" and treasure him. If the European Community bureaucrats have their way (as they seem determined to do) he will not be with us much longer. Under the increasing pressure of the regulations which stream out of Brussels daily, small family firms, both pork and red meat butchers, are being bludgeoned by economic factors into purchasing their meat from large factory processors, even though the quality of the meat is often inferior to that which they can produce themselves using the traditional methods. If they are finally forced to give in to this constant pressure and harassment the old craft of the butcher will be lost forever. Guilds of tradesmen have existed in Ireland since medieval times and along with 28 other guilds the butchers took part in the annual performances of the medieval Mystery Play cycles. The butchers always represented the *tormentours* of Christ "with their garmentis well and truly peinted." The Dublin Master Butchers Federation was formed 110 years ago and today The Irish Master Butchers Federation runs a variety of annual competitions to find the All-Ireland Champion in pudding making, sausage making and spiced beef preparation.

Bacon and Cabbage

There are few Irish families who do not cook this dish regularly.The usual cut they use is the shoulder, the collar, or a piece of unsliced streaky bacon from the flitch. In factory-cured bacon these cuts can be excessively salty and so the joint is usually soaked overnight in several changes of cold water and may even be brought to the boil for 5 minutes in the final change of water which is then discarded.

The joint is then put into a pot of fresh water along with some "pot herbs." Onion, celery, carrot, a bay leaf or two, parsley stalks, juniper berries, a dollop of sugar and a dash of vinegar are all common additions. The water is brought to the boil and then the heat reduced to a bare simmer and the joint cooked for 25-30 minutes per pound weight. It should be very tender.

It used to be that the cabbage was washed and sliced and added to the pot in which the bacon was cooking, often for an hour or more, but the modern taste for vegetables which are not murdered in this way dictates that it is more usual to take a cup of the liquid from the bacon pot and bring it back to the boil in a separate pot. The finely shredded cabbage is added to this and cooked very quickly until just barely tender.

If the whole joint is to be eaten hot then the skin is removed and the bacon sliced quite thickly. White parsley sauce and floury boiled, or steamed, potatoes (in their skins) are the traditional accompaniments and are very hard to beat. If part of the joint is to be kept for another meal then the skin is usually left on the joint and any meat not to be eaten at the sitting is put back into its cooking liquid to cool naturally. This keeps it moist and much tastier as a cold cut.

Baked Ham

This is a rather more aristocratic dish as the hams were, of course, the prime cuts of the pig. The hams were usually smoked. There are a variety of ways of doing this but the most famous, Limerick Ham, was smoked using juniper berries. Oak shavings were often used and there is an unusual mixture in this 18th-century recipe:

> "Hang in a chimney and make a fire of oak shavings and lay over it horse litter and one pound of juniper berries. Keep the fire smothered down for 2 or three days and then hang them to dry."

This comes from Florence Irwin's book *The Cookin' Woman*. She was a Domestic Science instructor in County Down at the turn of this century and for decades after that she wrote on cookery as a journalist and broadcaster. She gathered many traditional Ulster recipes and her book gives an insight into food commonly eaten there forty years ago.

Ham is cooked in exactly the same way as the bacon joint but is then baked in the oven for 30 to 40 minutes. The skin is removed for this and it is often given a decorative crust by patting dried breadcrumbs mixed with a little brown sugar over the layer of fat, which can also be studded with whole cloves. It is placed in a baking dish with a cup of cider or orange juice. It is baked until the crust is lightly browned.

Pickled Pork

This is increasingly available in city shops and popular in the poorer areas. Both belly pork and the hocks (shanks) are pickled in brine and are inexpensive to buy. The hock is usually cut generously and has a good bit of meat on it. The pork is put into a pot of cold water, brought slowly to the boil, skimmed well and simmered very gently for 1½ - 2 hours. Vegetables, commonly onions, carrots, celery, a small parsnip, occasionally some swede or turnip, are added about half an hour before the end of the cooking time to simmer with the meat until tender. Served with parsley sauce and steamed or boiled potatoes in their jackets.

Cruibeens

The pig's trotters, lightly brined, are highly prized, particularly after a feed of stout (Guinness, Murphy's or Beamish). The rear feet are favoured because there's supposed to be more meat on them but it's not for the meat that they are liked. They are rich, gelatinous, full of fat and devoured, as they say in Cork, "shkin an' all".

When I was a small child, in the centre of Dublin, an Italian family ran a fish-and-chip shop directly across from my father's pub. Only on Saturday nights, at pub closing-time, they served cruibeens from a separate window onto the street. As well as local men returning home from the city centre pubs after "a few jars," the window attracted all the dogs in the neighbourhood, who gathered in a semi-circle round the window waiting for the discarded bones which had been sucked clean by the customers. It was impossible to keep our usually well-behaved dog from joining this noisy throng. Food clearly fit for man and beast!

You will need 2-3 cruibeens per person. (This depends on their size, the appetite of the person and the amount of stout consumed beforehand.) Place the cruibeens in cold water along with onion and parsley stalks and some freshly ground black pepper. Bring them to the boil then turn down the heat and simmer them very gently until completely tender and falling from the bone. There are all kinds of ways of binding several trotters together with string to keep them from falling apart but they are all attempts to gild the lily. There is no elegant way of eating cruibeens. Use your fingers and suck. They are, it should be pointed out, an acquired taste, which many people are happy never to acquire. At home they should be served with brown soda cake, or griddle bread, and butter.

Tripe and Onions

Tripe is the stomach tissue of cud-chewing animals, usually beef, but sometimes veal (the best), and often pork. It is sold by butchers as dressed tripe, which means that it has been thoroughly cleaned and given a long initial cooking to tenderise it. The *honeycomb* patterned tripe of the second stomach is tenderer than the flat or ridged variety. Dressed tripe still requires a couple of hours more slow-cooking.

People either like tripe or hate it. I don't believe there is an in-between state. A lot of Irish people do like it very much. As *tripes à la mode de Caen* is one of the great peasant dishes of Norman France it is not unreasonable to believe that this liking for tripe is something the Normans brought with them to Ireland.

1 lb dressed honeycomb tripe
1 lb onions (peeled, chopped)
2 cups milk
pinch grated nutmeg
2 tbsp fresh chopped parsley
salt and freshly ground black pepper
4 tbsp cream
1 tsp cornflour

The tripes are cut into small 1-inch squares and brought to the boil in water. They are drained, placed in a suitable baking dish or casserole along with the onions, the milk (use just enough to cover), the nutmeg and seasoning. Cook, covered, in a slow oven at 160°C (325°F, Gas Mark 3) for at least 2 hours or until completely tender. Use any remaining milk to top up the liquid if it gets too dry. About 10 minutes before serving, remove the lid, and add the cornflour which should be mixed in 2 tablespoonsful of water. Stir it over a low heat until it thickens. Now add the cream and the chopped parsley. Return briefly to the oven to heat through (do not boil) before serving with wholemeal bread.

Dublin Coddle

I had tasted more dishes which purported to be "real Dubbelin coddle" than almost any other Irish dish and had reached the conclusion that Dean Swift must have been truly mad if it was his favourite food. Then, one day, I got, as they say, waylaid in a Dublin pub called The Long Hall. Somehow my companions and I got caught up in a funeral celebration. A lovely, elderly woman began to speak to me and, despite her advanced state of inebriation, maintained stoutly that "de chisullurs," (her children) "would be grand for grub dat night because der was a great pot of coddle on de stove." She further informed me, when I displayed interest in how she made it, that it was both "grub for a Saherda nite, and fur de funerals, cos it doesn't spoil if it's left for an hour or two too long." This is her recipe and now I know exactly why Jonathan Swift liked it so much.

1 lb bacon bits
1 lb of good meaty sausages
3 large onions
3-4 lb potatoes
a handful of fresh chopped parsley
freshly ground black pepper

Bacon bits are the off-cuts from the various types of bacon which are sold very cheaply in Dublin pork butchers'shops specifically for making coddle. They contain a good mixture of fat, lean and skin. I prefer to buy streaky bacon (the belly bacon) in the piece and cut it up into even-sized pieces. Leave on the skin as it adds great richness to the soup. Buy the finest quality pork sausages you can afford (or find). Peel and chop the onions roughly. Peel the potatoes as thinly as possible. If they are large then cut them into two or three large pieces, otherwise leave them whole. Chop the fresh parsley.

Place a layer of onions in the bottom of a heavy pot with a good close-fitting lid. Layer all the other ingredients, giving each layer a twist of freshly ground black pepper. Add no more than 2 cups of water to the pot. Bring the water to the boil then reduce the heat at once, cover tightly, and barely simmer for 2 to 5 hours. The perfect way to cook it is in a heavy casserole pot in a very low oven at 120°C (250°F, Gas Mark ½). I know this sounds very vague but if the pot is heavy and the lid tight it really cannot come to any harm. The longer and slower the cooking the better, in fact. If you prefer it, before serving, remove the sausages and quickly brown them on one side under the grill. Serve with white griddle bread to mop up the soup and bottles of stout. It is a most restorative food.

Brawn

It is increasingly difficult to buy a good brawn so if you want to taste this delicacy then you really must make it yourself. Traditionally, brawns would have been made from the head, shoulders and trotters of wild boar. But it used not to be uncommon for brawns, or head cheeses, to be made from calves' head, sheep's head or a mixture of several meats. Pigs' heads are sold in centre city and country pork butchers but hardly ever in suburban ones. I wonder why! The head should have been lightly brined for 24 hours and should have the tongue intact for preference. Brawn will keep well for up to 2 weeks in a fridge and should not be deep-frozen because the jelly partially liquefies when it defrosts. A whole head will make a lot of brawn and so I give the recipe for a half-head. In this case try and buy a whole tongue separately. Check the pickle strength with the butcher. If it is heavily salted then soak the head overnight and wipe it thoroughly before cooking. The brain and eyes can be removed by the butcher.

½ pig's head
1 pig's tongue
2 cruibeens (trotters)
1 large onion (peeled, sliced)
1 carrot (sliced)
1 stick celery (sliced)
1 cup dry cider
3-4 bay leaves
sprigs of thyme
sprigs of parsley
Bunch of celery leaves
6 whole peppercorns
¼ tsp grated nutmeg
freshly ground black pepper

Chop the head into manageable pieces but retain the tongue in one piece. Put them in a large pot with the trotters, the vegetables, the herbs and spices (not the nutmeg) and the tongue. Add the cider and then enough cold water to cover. Bring it to the boil, skimming it frequently. Reduce the heat and simmer gently for 2-3 hours or until the meat is very tender. Remove the head pieces and the tongue. Allow them to cool, putting the tongue into cold water. When both are cool strip the meat from the head bones and the skin from the tongue. Cut off the root from the tongue but keep the tongue in one piece. Strain the stock and return it to the pan to boil and reduce by half its volume. Season the remaining liquid with salt and freshly ground black pepper and return the meat to the pan with the nutmeg. Simmer for about 10 minutes. Rinse a suitable bowl or mould with cold water and place all the meat from the pan into it. Place the whole tongue in the centre. Pour enough of the liquid from the pan over the meat until it is just covered. Place in a cool place overnight to cool or in a refrigerator covered with a piece of foil. It will set firmly. Some people like to press the brawn but I have never found it really necessary. Turn out onto a serving plate and garnish with sprigs of fresh parsley. Cut into slices as you need it. It is delicious with crisp green salads, a good mustard and wholemeal bread.

Drisheen

Black or blood puddings are eaten all over Ireland but only in Cork and parts of Kerry, where they take their puddings seriously, are they called *drisheen*. In the Cork covered market there is even a specialist shop which sells nothing but drisheen and tripe. Mind you, there are differences in the size and the shape of the skins used to encase puddings and occasionally, particularly in Cork City, the *drisheen* is not put into a skin at all but cooked in a bowl. The basic ingredients of all black puddings are blood, fat, milk or cream, and some kind of cereal, herb or spice, and seasoning. In the very earliest times the blood would have been cow's, later it might have been sheep's, and today it is almost invariably pig's blood.

The recipes vary a great deal, from region to region, often from butcher to butcher in the same small town; what will delight a Wexford man will leave a Galway woman unmoved and a Dubliner of either sex feeling that it leaves a great deal to be desired. Each year the Master Butchers competitions are hotly contested. I have been judging these competitions for quite a number of years now and know what I like in a pudding. But I must freely acknowledge that my husband likes something quite different. I offer the following recipe simply because it is one that you can make at home. But if you develop or already have a taste for this princely dish then you must experiment until you find a combination of fat size, cereal, herbs and spices which suits your taste. Obviously you need to be on good terms with a pork butcher who still kills his own pigs in order to get a supply of blood.

5 cups of pig's blood
1 tsp salt to keep the blood liquid
2 onions finely chopped
2½ cups cream
2 cups pinhead oatmeal
1 tsp chopped fresh tansy leaves
1 tsp freshly ground black pepper
1-2 tsp mixture of allspice, nutmeg, cinnamon
pinch of ground cloves
1 lb fat (flair or back)

The salt is added to the blood and stirred while it is cooling. This keeps it liquid. If a pint of cream seems too rich then you can, if you must, use a half-and-half mixture of cream and milk. The fat too is a matter of preference. The flair fat is the membranous fat which surrounds the kidneys and forms the lining of the loin. When heated it tends to melt down completely. The back fat is cut into a dice; the size depends upon personal taste, but you might start with one which gives you cubes of fat of roughly one-third of an inch. These will not render down as much as the flair during cooking. The balance of spices in the mixture is a matter for experiment as well. Tansy can be difficult to get now unless you grow it yourself and it is quite common nowadays for thyme to be substituted. This is absolutely forbidden if you want a real Cork City drisheen.

Render about a quarter of the fat in a pan and add the onion to it. Gently fry the onion until it is very soft but not browned. Now mix together thoroughly all the ingredients apart from the blood. Finally stir in the blood. You can, of course, put this mixture into skins, if you can get them, but it is, for home use, much simpler to put the lot into a well-greased baking dish. Cover and place it in a roasting tin half-full of water. Place this in a pre-heated slow oven at 150°C (325°F, Gas Mark 3) until it is set and not exuding blood when tested with a skewer. This will take from 1-1½ hours. When it has cooled completely, turn it out and cut it into serving slices which can be eaten cold, fried for breakfast, or just warmed in the oven and served with a good white onion sauce.

Onion Sauce

1 lb onions (peeled, chopped fine)
½ tsp salt
2 tbsp melted butter
1½ tbsp flour
2 cups milk or stock
½ cup fresh cream
freshly ground black pepper
⅛ tsp grated nutmeg

Cook the finely chopped onions very gently, with the salt, in the butter until they are really soft but not browned. Add the flour and cook, stirring all the time, for 3 minutes. Away from the heat, add the milk or stock which has been heated to just below boiling temperature. Whisk it all the time while adding it to prevent lumps forming. Simmer the sauce over a low heat for 10 minutes. Thin the thickened sauce with the cream and season with the pepper and the nutmeg. You can, if you prefer, purée the sauce but this would not normally be considered necessary. Serve very hot with black pudding.

An Irish Breakfast

In Ulster this is known, rather obviously, as an Ulster Fry and in some other parts of the country it is known, rather quaintly, as a *cooked* breakfast.

No matter where you eat it, properly constituted, it should consist of bacon rashers, black and white pudding, pork sausages, fried egg, fried potato cakes or bread, fried tomatoes and, in season, field mushrooms. It is eaten with brown soda bread and butter and a large pot of strong tea. There are no *ifs* and *buts* about this—the Irish breakfast is a far more serious affair than your common or garden bacon and eggs. For each person served you will need two rashers of bacon—one of them back bacon, the other streaky—two pork sausages, a piece of white and a piece of black pudding, at least one fried egg, a whole tomato halved, and one potato cake or slice of bread to be fried in the bacon fat. (In really supreme Irish breakfasts the fried bread is always white griddle soda bread.) Only the mushrooms are optional. There is a case to be made for adding a half pork or lamb's kidney and some liver, and I have seen a juicy lamb chop sneak in if the woman of the house thought you needed "feeding up." If the breakfast didn't kill you, you were set up for the day. Until quite recently all this was cooked in an enormous, blackened iron frying pan, kept specially for the breakfast. Now the rashers, sausages, tomatoes and sometimes the puddings are more likely to be grilled.

Skirts and Kidneys

I had heard references to this famous dish from Cork but knew that it was rarely eaten today. Thanks to the detective powers of Phyll O'Kelly, food writer with the *Cork Examiner* newspaper, I received a recipe from Poppy Loughran, a Cork lady renowned for her cooking. The skirt is the diaphragm of the pig and is rarely sold today but put into sausages. Any help-ful butcher will take an order in advance for them. The same cut is available from beef and lamb. But this dish is always made from pork.

  1 lb pork skirts
  1-2 pork kidneys
  1 large onion (peeled, sliced)
  1-2 carrots (peeled, sliced)
  1 tsp cornflour

Trim the skin, membrane and fat from the skirts and the kidneys. Halve, core and then thinly slice the kidneys and put them to soak in cold water for 2 hours. Drain them and dry them. Place all the ingredients in a heavy pot or casserole with barely enough water to cover. Season with salt and freshly ground black pepper, bring to the boil and then cover the pot and simmer for 1 hour. Thicken the juices with the cornflour and add a good handful of fresh chopped parsley just before serving. Boiled potatoes—the classic accompaniment.

Bodices

A bodice, for those of you too young to remember, was an inner garment for the upper part of the body, strengthened with whalebone ribs. The bodices of this dish are bacon ribs and the body they support is a soft, tasty potato stuffing. Once again I have to thank Poppy Loughran for the recipe.

You will need two whole sheets of bacon ribs each divided into two pieces. Place the two smaller half-sheets of rib in the bottom of a suitable baking dish with the thin ends of the rib to the centre of the dish. Spread the potato stuffing over these ribs and then place the remaining ribs to cover it. Bake in a pre-heated oven at 200°C (400°F, Gas Mark 6) for 1½ hours. The ribs should be brown and crisp.

Divide into 4 servings and eat the ribs with your fingers and the potato stuffing with a spoon. Gentility goes out of the window with bodices in the same way that it does with *cruibeens*.

Beef

The modern notion of fattening cattle to slaughtering weight in eighteen months to three years was unheard of in Ireland until quite recent times. Cattle were slaughtered at anything up to seven years when they were beyond milk production or use as draught animals. Irish cattle were small breeds and it was not until the 18th century that the larger breeds were introduced and later still that the cattle from the west of the country began to be driven to the rich grasslands of County Meath to be fattened. The Vikings actually introduced their own "red" cattle to interbread with the Irish stock. These "red polls" were still a distinctive bread near Crayabbey in Co. Down up to 1934.

In any event, most Irish cattle were exported, some on the hoof, but a great deal of them as salted beef—corned beef as we know it. This was the only beef that ordinary Irish people ate, except on rare feast-days like Christmas, when a strong farmer who might slaughter a cow sent out a joint to his neighbours—the beef equivalent of the pudding round. Fresh beef was often cooked in the pot oven in exactly the same way as salted beef.

Corned Beef and Cabbage

2-3 lb corned beef
1 onion
1 carrot
bay leaf, parsley and thyme
2 cloves of garlic
1 cup cider
a large head of green cabbage

The most usual cuts used for corning today are brisket and the tail-end but if you can get a silverside then grab it. The salt-petre used in the pickle has a tendency to toughen the meat so corned beef needs long, slow, careful cooking if it is not to become stringy and tough. This, sadly, is knowledge that has been forgotten by many Irish cooks and I have had too many plates of tough corned beef in restaurants and pubs all over Ireland.

Soak the meat overnight in several changes of cold water. Clean, peel and chop the vegetables roughly and place them and the pot herbs into the pot or casserole with the meat. It should be a snug fit. Pour over the cider and enough water to cover the meat completely. Bring to the boil, skimming all the time. Reduce the heat so that the water is barely simmering. Cover tightly and cook in a pre-heated oven at 150°C (300°F, Gas Mark 2) for 42 minutes per pound weight. Test it for tenderness when three-quarters of the cooking time has elapsed as you might have been lucky and got really tender meat. Serve hot with lightly boiled cabbage and white parsley sauce (or the mustard sauce in the following recipe) and steamed potatoes in their jackets.

Mustard Sauce

Mustard was always a popular spice in Ireland because it is one of the few which can be grown successfully here. Coarsely ground mustard seeds were often the only savour available for potatoes. This sauce is good with both spiced and corned beef as well as being a traditional accompaniment to herrings.

    2 tbsp melted butter
    ½ tbsp flour
    2 cups milk
    1 tbsp wine or cider vinegar
    1 tsp sugar
    salt and freshly ground black pepper to taste
    1 tbsp coarsely ground mustard seed
        (this could be English mustard powder or, better still, an Irish coarse mustard with honey or whiskey)

Melt the butter in a saucepan and stir in the flour. Cook gently for a minute or two then whisk in the milk and simmer for 3 minutes. Blend in the rest of the ingredients and stir well until mixed. Serve hot.

Spiced Beef

Spices, although imported into the country from very early times, were luxuries and so this dish was for feasting rather than for everyday. It is quite a lot of trouble to prepare at home and so, apart from being a Christmas treat, it rather fell out of favour. But interest in it has revived in recent times. For the last few years there has been an annual, hotly contested competition for butchers held during the Ashford Show in County Wicklow. This is the big pre-Christmas meat sale in early December. As one of the regular judges for this spiced beef competition I know that the regular winning entrants do produce excellent spiced beefs and, if you're lucky enough to live near them, there is no need to go further. But some of the entrants are still unwilling to spend the time necessary to produce the genuine article.

Every competent cook has her own special spice mixture and they do vary wildly. Florence Irwin's Ulster recipe has thirteen different ingredients but others are happy with five or six. Two Irish cooks whom I respect a great deal, Myrtle Allen and Honor Moore, use more or less the same mixture of spices. Myrtle Allen of Ballymaloe House has done more than almost anyone else to revive a pride in Irish ingredients cooked simply and well, both at her country house hotel in County Cork and in Paris, where the *La Ferme Irlandaise* restaurant had queues out into the street when she ran it. Honor Moore, food writer and journalist, regularly spices her own beef, says she has used several methods over the years but always comes back to this method in the end. Both base their spice mixture on allspice, juniper berries, black pepper and sugar. Mrs. Allen uses slightly more sugar and because I prefer a slightly less sweet mixture this is Honor Moore's recipe.

4-5 lb beef (rump, brisket, tail-end, silverside or round)
½ oz saltpetre
8 oz sea salt
1 oz whole black peppercorns
1 oz allspice
12 whole dried juniper berries
pinch of ground cloves
3 oz brown sugar
2 bay leaves

Mix the salt and the saltpetre and rub some of it well into the meat. Leave the salt on the meat and leave it, covered, in a cool place. Each day, for 4 days, rub some of this mixture into every crevice of the meat. Grind all the whole spices and mix them together thoroughly with the brown sugar and a good pinch of ground cloves. You should have very little of the salt left by now. On the 5th day, in a clean dish, place the salted meat into the mixed spices. Rub these well into the flesh. Store covered in a cool place. Every second day over 10-14 days repeat this process of rubbing in the spices.

Before cooking, tie a large branch of fresh thyme, several bay leaves, and a few whole cloves to the meat with a strip of cloth. Simmer in water to which has been added 2 cups of stout, an onion, a carrot and some parsley. Some people dislike the taste of the stout so it can be omitted. It is cooked exactly as for corned beef, barely simmered, for 42-45 minutes per pound. It can be eaten hot but it is more usual to serve it cold, after a light pressing during cooling, sliced very thinly. In our family it is always accompanied by pickled pears, sweet pickled onions or cauliflower, and good homemade bread.

Collared Fat Ribs of Beef

From Elizabethan times onwards there are many references to Collared Beef in which the word could mean either a neck collar or the method of wrapping rolled meat tightly in a cloth to preserve its shape during cooking. In later times, in Ireland, the term seems to have been interpreted as a roll of spiced beef served on a plate surrounded, as a garnish, by a "collar" of cooked vegetables.

However, I recently came across the following recipe from a book of "receipts" published in 1828, in which the meat is corned and stuffed before being wrapped in the cloth for cooking. The finished dish does indeed resemble the stiff, pleated Elizabethan ruff or decorative neck collar and so may indeed explain the coincidence of the two terms. It certainly looks very pretty on the plate. The meat is treated in a manner which is a cross between plain corned (salted) beef and spiced beef. It is hardly worth going to the trouble with a piece of boned and rolled fat rib of less than 6-8 lb.

6-8 lb boned rib of beef
6 oz brown sugar
4 oz salt
1 oz saltpetre
3 cups fresh chopped parsley
3 cups finely chopped fat pork
3 cups breadcrumbs
½ tsp ground mace
pinch ground nutmeg
¼ tsp ground black pepper
½ tsp salt

The Irish have always liked a goodly portion of fat on their meat, believing rightly that this improves the flavour during cooking. The recipe works best with a boned rib of beef which has a good layer of fat and plenty of marbling. In deference to modern taste you could trim this fat.

Grind together the sugar with 4 oz salt and the saltpetre so that they are thoroughly mixed. Rub this mixture into the meat all over the surface. Let it remain in this pickle for 10 days, turning it over each day. After 10 days remove the meat from the pickle and soak it for 6-8 hours in cold water. Remove it and dry it thoroughly. Place the meat on a flat surface with the outer skin down. With a sharp knife cut slits lengthways in the

111

meat to the depth of about an inch in the thickest part of the joint and slightly less as you get to the thinner section.

Mix the ground mace, salt, pepper and nutmeg with the breadcrumbs. Fill the first slit with the chopped parsley, the next with the finely chopped fat pork, and the third with the spiced breadcrumbs. Repeat this sequence until you have filled all the slits and used up your stuffings. Now roll up the meat as tightly as you are able and tie it. Wrap the tied joint in a clean cloth and then bind it with coarse tape. Place it in a pot with enough water to cover and bring it to the boil. Turn it down to a slow simmer immediately and cook for 4-5 hours depending on the weight. Remove the meat from the pot and place it on a flat surface. Place a flat board and weights on top and press the meat until it is cold. Remove the cloths and the string. Serve cold as for spiced beef.

Beef Stew

There is nothing very special about this stew except that a common addition to beef stews in Ireland is stout or ale instead of stock or water. Originally this would have been entirely dependent upon whether the brewery nearest you made stout or beer. Like all Irish stews it is eaten with mounds of floury potatoes. In Dublin, certainly, the preferred cut would be shin beef because, given long, slow cooking (a gentle simmering only), it softens to a melting tenderness and produces a thick, rich, gelatinous gravy.

1-1½ lb shin beef
2 large onions (peeled,chopped)
2-3 carrots
1 oz butter or beef dripping
pot herbs (bay, parsley, thyme)
1 cup stout or beer
1 cup water
salt and freshly ground black pepper

Melt the fat in a large frying pan and fry the onions gently until they are translucent and beginning to brown at the edges. Remove them with a slotted spoon and place them with the sliced carrots in the bottom of a casserole. Remove the outer membrane from the shin beef and any large sinews. Cut the meat into rounds about an inch thick and brown them quickly in the hot fat to seal them. Remove the meat from the pan and place it in the casserole on top of the carrots and onions. Deglaze the pan with the stout or beer. Add this liquid to the casserole along with the water, pot herbs and seasoning. Cover tightly and cook slowly in a pre-heated oven at 160°C (325°F, Gas Mark 3) for 3 hours. Like all Irish stews this is a flexible dish, capable of many embellishments. You may need to thicken the gravy with flour if you use a cut other than shin beef. (This should be done by dusting the meat pieces in seasoned flour before sealing it in the frying pan.) It can be further enriched by the addition of ox or lamb's kidney and it improves in flavour if allowed to cool before being re-heated in a day or two.

Mutton and Lamb

In Ireland sheep were kept primarily for their wool and, of course, they were milked. In ancient times there are very few references to the eating of sheep meat. In truth, it was probably eaten only when misadventure shortened the life of a beast. Certainly that modern favourite, prime tender young lamb, was a rarity.

In spite of this, Irish Stew is probably our best-known dish beyond these shores. But then again, properly prepared, Irish stew will make a good meal of the most ancient auld ewe. There is a tradition which claims that the original meat for an Irish stew was the meat of the goat. It would make sense because there were always domesticated goats in Ireland. We still have wild goats, and a proportion of bones from goats have been found in the earliest cooking sites and habitations.

E. Estyn Evans claims that the goat, along with the donkey, became a symbol of poverty in post-famine Ireland and so despised that the keeping of goats and the making of goat's milk cheese died out. Yet the goat is the ideal animal to graze much of the rough hill pasture so abundant and underused in Ireland today. It is making something of a comeback. Many smallholders, committed to living the self-sufficient good life, have begun to produce excellent goat's cheese, milk and yoghurt. While an old goat is still pretty unpalatable and better treated, as one book has it, "like bad venison," young, tender kid is a delicate meat and now beginning to be available once more.

However, though I have had an Irish stew made from young kid (and delicious it was), Irish Stew is normally made from either mutton or lamb. Mutton is essential, say the purists. But then I've never been a dogmatic purist and, quite simply, I prefer lamb. This could be because of unpleasant memories of perpetual boiled mutton in my days at boarding-school. Modern Irish chefs have transformed this quintessential white stew into an often complicated and refined dish but the basic recipe is not to be despised for that. It is its very simplicity which makes it so enduring.

Irish Stew

> 1½ lb stewing lamb or mutton (this might be
>   shoulder, neck, gigot chops or trimmed breast)
> 2 large onions
> 3 lb potatoes
> large bunch fresh parsley
> 2 tsp chopped fresh thyme
> water
> salt and freshly ground black pepper

Most Irish people consider that the fat and bones are an integral part of Irish Stew. The fat is absorbed by the potatoes and the meat is cooked until the meat falls away from the bones which enrich the gravy and do not pose a hazard. Peel the onions and slice them into rounds. Peel the potatoes as thinly as possible. Leave them whole unless they are very large. Cut the meat into good-sized pieces. Small gigot chops can be left whole, larger ones divided in two. Place a layer of onions on the bottom of a heavy pot or casserole and the meat on top of them. Sprinkle chopped thyme and parsley generously and season well. Layer the rest of the onions with the potatoes. Sprinkle thyme and parsley at the last. The amount of water you need to add depends upon how good the seal is between your pot and its lid, and whether you like a "wet" or a dry stew. You will certainly not need more than two cups and I use barely one. Bring the water to the boil, cover as tightly as possible, and place in a pre-heated oven at 150°C (300°F, Gas Mark 2) for 2½-3 hours. Keep an eye on it towards the end and adjust the gravy by adding a little more water if you think it too dry. A good Irish stew should have some gravy but should not be flooded with it. Floury potatoes will dissolve into the gravy, waxy ones will not. Which you use is a matter of choice. I tend to use a mixture. Serve very hot with more fresh chopped parsley sprinkled on top. White griddle bread to mop up the gravy.

Goose

Traditionally goose was eaten on two days of the year, at Michaelmas and at Christmas. Indeed, the goose vied with beef as the main dish on the table for Christmas Day.

The wild barnacle goose was the object of one of those hilarious medieval misconceptions which maintained that it came not from eggs but from shellfish which grow from water-logged wood in the sea. "Accordingly," says Gerald of Wales in his *History and Topography of Ireland* (which he wrote in the early part of the 12th century), "in some parts of Ireland bishops and religious men eat them without sin during a fasting time, regarding them as not being flesh, since they were not born of flesh." This traditional benefit of clergy is reputed to have persisted in Tralee, County Kerry, until very recent times even though Pope Innocent III forbade the practice in 1215. Kerry men obviously believe in having their goose and eating it!

Michaelmas, from Norman times, was in some parts of the country a hiring day or rent day. In Carlow in 1305 a goose was worth twenty old pennies and the landlord would accept the money or a goose as his rent. In later times Michaelmas became one of the days of the year on which farmers killed an animal and gave food to their poorer neighbours. It was very often a goose, or two, from the large flocks kept by their wives which they killed. In the apple-growing areas of Ireland, Munster and South Ulster, this was the day on which the apple harvest began, a time to make cider to serve with a goose and baked apples.

Nothing of the goose was wasted. Its quills were made into writing implements and fishing floats, the down and feathers used in mattresses and pillows, and its fat, goose grease, rubbed into the chest as a cure for "chestiness." This remedy was still in use when I was a child. Recently it was suggested to me by a countrywoman as a cure for tennis elbow or for tendonitis of any kind. I've also seen this wonderful fat wasted on a big black kitchen range to "bring up the shine." I suppose what I'm really saying is that in the matter of the goose, we Irish can teach the French absolutely nothing. And yet, for me, Christmas is not complete without roast goose stuffed with potato and onion. As a Christmas food it has declined here, replaced by the intensively reared turkey. Down the years, it would have been cooked in a bastible oven with cider and apples but it is now an expensive luxury. But the goose fat is wonderful for cooking potatoes with for the rest of the year!

CHAPTER FIVE
THE POTATO

In the space of one hundred years, between 1741 and 1841, the population of this island increased from 3 million to 8 million. During this period, for the vast majority of the people, the potato became almost the only daily food.

This may seem an astonishing growth rate at first. However, you should remember that in Ireland today the population is around 3½, but it remains more or less static only as a result of the emigration of roughly 40,000 young people a year. If they were to stay here and half of them were women, of whom half might marry and produce two children, then the next century would see an increase in population of a similar magnitude. It is perfectly clear to us now that we could not support such a population, given the present economic and social structures. But if we remember that, at the beginning of the period in question, there was work and food for all, it becomes easier to understand, if not to condone, the birth rate of the Irish during the 18th and 19th centuries.

Towards the end of the 18th century there was an enormous market for Irish grain in Europe. European agriculture had collapsed after decades of wars, culminating in the Napoleonic wars. Irish farmers, especially in the south-east, put a vast acre-age under tillage to meet this demand. This provided work for large numbers of labourers who were very often provided with a plot of land and the grazing of a cow, as well as a wage. As the population increased, the potato was the crop which the labourers cultivated to support their growing families. In Ulster and north Connaught there was a flourishing cottage industry in spinning, weaving and sprigging which provided work for women and girls as well as the men. This income allowed them to pay the rent of a small plot of land on which to grow the potato and keep a pig. These two areas held the largest proportion of the population. In the western half of the country the traditional form of farming, on the Rundale system, could provide for larger families—provided that they lived on the potato. In turn, the potato, with milk, some vegetables and some, occasional, meat or fish, provided a relatively healthy diet which was a cause, according to some historians, of an increase in health and fertility. People were living longer. And, as can be seen the world over in countries without state welfare systems, a large family was considered a way of ensuring that the parents would be cared for in old age.

Whether it was the increase in population which forced a dependence upon the potato, or whether the potato's abundant crop caused the increase in population, is an academic argument. The result of this growing dependence upon the potato is plain to see. When, after the Battle of Waterloo, a degree of stability was restored to continental Europe, the markets for Irish grain contracted rapidly. The conditions which had supported the increased population of Ireland changed over a very short period of time. The landlords reverted to the production of sheep and cattle, the demand for labour contracted almost overnight, forcing wages down dramatically. The peasant workers were unable to pay the rents on their potato patches and the grazing for their cow, and their holdings became smaller and smaller. Cut off from milk and an income from their butter and pigs, they were forced to rely more and more upon the potato as almost their only food. The industrial revolution in Britain's textile industry had an equally devastating effect on the cottage industry in Ulster and Connaught. The textile workers here were left without income and forced to rely on their potato patch. The Rundale system of land management in the West collapsed under the strains imposed upon it by increasing population.

The Rundale system was based around a group of houses, a *clachan*, surrounded by a large arable area held in common, a common pasturage—the outfield, and the rough mountain grazing and bog. Each household in the *clachan* had rights to a portion of each type of land, usually allocated by the annual drawing of lots. By the 19th century, when the system survived only on marginal lands, the increased population, combined with an inheritance system which subdivided the rights to the land between all the children in a kin group, resulted in a total breakdown of a system which, even at the best of times, did little to encourage the maintenance of fertility in the land. The situation reached its ultimate futility in Mayo and Donegal. At Rathlackan, in Mayo, 56 families occupied land scattered and divided into 1500 fragments. A landlord in Donegal around 1840 wrote that "one poor man, who had his inheritance in 32 different places, abandoned them in utter despair of ever being able to make them out." Ireland was heading for disaster but few in power cared.

There were a number of famines before the Great Famine of 1847. Few of the landlords or politicians seemed inclined to take note. In 1834 William Cobbett, a blunt Englishman with little time for the politics and social structures of his own country, pleaded for a repeal of the Act of Union of Gt. Britain and Ireland:

"There is a famine to a greater or lesser extent every year . . . of these ordinary, annual famines the English people hear nothing at all; but we have had since The Union, which was to make the Irish so happy, THREE GRAND FAMINES and here is a spectacle such as this world never beheld except in Ireland. What did it behold? Hundreds of thousands of living hogs; thousands upon thousands of sheep and oxen alive; thousands upon thousands of barrels of beef, pork and butter; thousands upon thousands of sides of bacon and thousands upon thousands of hams; ship loads and boat loads coming daily and hourly from Ireland to feed the West of Scotland; to feed the million and a half people in the West Riding of Yorkshire and in Lancashire; to feed London and its vicinity and to fill the country shops in the southern counties of England: we beheld this while famine raged in Ireland amongst the raisers of this very food."

Cobbett also defended the Irish against the charge of laziness and indolence which was levelled against them by defenders of the status quo, pointing out that Ireland provisioned British North America, the West Indies, the East Indies, The British Navy and parts of the Mediterranean.

"Can it be a lazy people who feed the world? Can it be a good government, under whose laws and regulations this laborious people are living upon roots, weeds or half-stinking mussels . . . No! Every reasonable man in this world will exclaim no it cannot be a good government."

But then Cobbett did not consider the potato to be a fit food for a working man and considered its introduction the chief burden under which the Irish laboured. He was equally vehement about the replacing of beer, in the working man's breakfast, by tea. Yet potatoes, in the Irish climate, would yield 9 tons to the acre, enough to feed 6 adult men for a year at the rate of 8 pounds a day. No grain crop could come near this.

In good years the potato crop would last a family for eleven months of the year. Even in those years when the crop did not fail, the month of July was a time of want. If they had the means they purchased oats or barley, if not they lived on wild herbage—nettles and charlock (*praiseach*). As a sole food charlock is unwholesome and turned their complexions as yellow as the flowers of the plant. The clergy recognised it as poor food and banned it in some places. July became known as "the yellow month," "hungry July" or "staggering July."

In coastal areas they were able to gather seaweeds and shellfish. There was little tradition of offshore fishing and fishermen relied upon the shoals of fish which came inshore in season. Coastal communities did eat a certain amount of fish and for that reason fared better than those inland; but the generality regarded fish more as a savour for potatoes than as a food in itself. Yet in a land teeming with inland lakes full of fish it is staggering that so little use was made of them to alleviate hunger in famine times. Perhaps it was the lack of boats or the means to build them which accounts for this.

Certainly most of the inland lakes at this time were in the hands of the great landowners who enforced savage game laws. If a poacher of hares or rabbits was caught he faced seven years' transportation to the colonies. And the Irish attitude to fish was compounded by the Church regulations on fasting which had induced an attitude in the people that fish was "penance" food.

It is difficult today to imagine how the countryside looked just before the Great Famine of 1847. The estates of the great landowners would still have been wooded to a degree and strong farmers would have had a shelter belt of trees. But the rest of the countryside had been stripped of anything that might be burnt as fuel, with endless potato ridges stretching as far as the eye could see and little else. Patrick Kavanagh, describing the potato fields of County Monaghan long after the famine, describes them as a thing of beauty:

> *The flocks of green potato-stalks*
> *Were blossom spread for sudden flight,*
> *The Kerr's Pinks in a frivelled blue,*
> *The Arran Banners wearing white.*

But when the blight struck, a potato crop, which looked healthy in the field, turned black in days and within a few weeks the tubers themselves became a rotten putrefying mass. Blight was not the result of the gradual impoverishment of the land, the lack of real crop rotation, or the dearth of animal manure to spread on the land, though all of these factors would have caused problems in any attempt to switch away from the dependence upon the potato. Blight is a fungal disease which thrives in the damp, humid weather endemic in Ireland. It can overwinter in the seed crop and, in the absence of anti-fungal sprays and resistant seed crops, it was impossible to control. For three years out of four in the mid-1840s the blight raged through the countryside causing famine beyond the imagination of even the far-sighted Cobbett.

About 1½ million people died of starvation, cholera and the fevers which followed it; another million emigrated and were followed by millions of others over the next hundred years. This population haemorrhage has been successfully halted only for a brief period in the sixties and seventies of this century. Yet, even with a population down below 4 million once more, we find it impossible to sustain our people at home. In the oft-repeated phrase of an Irish farmer, "We rear one for the farm and the rest for the world."

Despite all of this, the potato is today as important in the Irish diet as rice is to the Chinese, or pasta to the Italians. Most Irish people eat potatoes once a day, many eat them twice. It is a very versatile food. Before the famines a wide range of potato dishes were generally eaten. Potatoes were combined with different vegetables, dressed with milk or butter, made into soups, breads, cakes and pastries and the recipes showed respect and understanding of them. The potato was always cooked in its jacket the better to preserve its nutrients. When I was a snotty-nosed jackeen child in Dublin we thought it great hilarity to chant this little rhyme at people up from Cork:

> *Do you ate potatoes?*
> *Bedad, I do.*
> *How do you ate them?*
> *Shhkin an' all!*
> *Do they choke you?*
> *Yerra, not at all!*

Whether you ate the skins or put them in the pig bucket everyone went to a great deal of trouble to ensure that the potatoes were "floury." It didn't matter if you came from the north and called them "praties," or from the south and called them "spuds," the floury varieties were the most highly prized and if they were not naturally floury you found a way of cooking them which brought out the best in them.

In country areas the potatoes were tipped into a flat osier basket or *skib* from which the cooking moisture could escape quickly. This was used as a communal self-service plate at table. In grander households they used potato *rings* in which a linen napkin was placed to absorb the moisture. These rings became quite elaborate in Georgian times and were often delicately worked with silver. Today, when the potatoes have been boiled, they are drained and a clean cloth is placed over them in the pan and they are returned to the heat to dry out before being served in an ordinary serving dish.

Potatoes tend to be eaten today as an accompaniment to other foods and many of the old dishes are no longer made. You will rarely, if ever, be served these in hotels or restaurants. Instead you will normally get a swift choice of potatoes boiled, baked, roasted or french-fried; or, in the up-market "atin' houses" you will be offered international potato dishes with an emphasis on the French way with potatoes (which usually demands potatoes which are anything but floury. This is a great shame. We had our own ways with the spud which are still delicious.

Mind you! I hold the farmers responsible for much of this, as they seem hell-bent on growing potatoes for the size of the crop rather than its quality. As a result, most of the older varieties are unavailable, having been replaced, like tomatoes, by varieties which produce a standard-sized, regularly shaped item, ideal for packing into plastic bags by machine, but fit only for chips!

Potatoes

Boiled Potatoes

The Irish always boil potatoes without peeling them—in their skins as they say—and this is nutritionally sound because most of the vitamins and minerals of the tubers are held just below the skin. If you peel the potatoes before cooking them you will, as we also say, lose all the goodness. You will also lose much of the taste. Even if it is your intention to mash the potatoes or process them further, it is better to peel them after cooking, when the skin can usually be peeled away as a very thin membrane.

In coastal areas potatoes were boiled, by preference, in sea water. Inland, or if you are doubtful about the quality of the sea near you, boil them in heavily salted water. The salt prevents the skins from cracking during boiling, protecting the potatoes from absorbing water, and the skins in their turn prevent too much salt being absorbed during cooking. The Irish prefer "floury" potatoes like Kerr's Pinks, Golden Wonders, King Edwards, or Records. Local names for these varieties may vary but if you ask for a "floury" potato you won't go too far wrong. Always try to buy potatoes free from skin blemishes and discoloration and to cook potatoes of a uniform size together.

Scrub the outer skin of the potatoes well with a stiff brush and put them into a pot which is large enough to hold them without overcrowding. Cover them with heavily salted water. For new potatoes use boiling water but for old potatoes use cold water. Bring the water to a boil then reduce the heat and cover the pot. The potatoes should just simmer. Cooking times are entirely dependent upon the size and type of the potatoes. Test them carefully with a very fine, metal skewer but not too often or, despite the salted water, the skins will break on you. When they are cooked, drain off the water and cover the potatoes in the pot with a clean absorbent cloth. Place the pot back on a very low heat to dry the potatoes for several minutes.

Plain boiled potatoes are peeled at the table if you are not going to eat them skin and all. The Irish way is to spear a potato with your fork and peel the skin off with a knife onto a side-plate. Eat them with butter or a herb-flavoured butter. Chopped fresh mint is particularly good with new potatoes.

Champ, Poundies, Stampy, Cally and Pandy

All of these dishes are variations on boiled, mashed potatoes with additions. The additions are most commonly members of the onion family like chives, scallions (spring onions) or ordinary onions. In the northern counties champ is also the name given to various other mixtures of mashed potatoes with beans, peas, parsley or nettles. Another similar dish made most often with kale, but sometimes with cooked cabbage, is known as colcannon. As it needs slightly more preparation I give a separate recipe.

    2-2½ lb of potatoes
    1 cup chopped scallions (spring onions)
    1 cup milk
    butter

Prepare boiled potatoes and while they are drying prepare the scallions. Chop the scallions, including the green leaves, and simmer them in the milk for a few minutes. Keep them warm while you "pound" the potatoes.

A pounder was a heavy block of wood on a long handle. It was used, often by the man of the house, to pound or stamp the spuds. Remember that it was quite usual in those days to cook half a stone (7 lb) of potatoes for each person so this could be quite heavy work. Whatever modern appliance you use it is essential to have a purée of potatoes completely free from lumps. Add the scallions and the milk to the mashed potatoes, season well with salt and freshly ground black pepper and mix them together thoroughly. You may add more milk if the mixture is not creamy enough but on no account add so much that they become wet.

Champ should be served piping hot, so it may be necessary to re-heat the potatoes at this point. Serve on very hot plates. Make a "dunt" in the top of the potatoes. This is for your butter which melts into a little lake on the top so that you can dip each spoonful of potato into it. Champ was, of course, a dish in itself but nowadays it is quite usual to serve it as an accompaniment to grilled sausages or boiled bacon. It is a perfect accompaniment for all kinds of fish.

Chives, small young nettle-tops, peas, broad beans, or 4-5 heaped tablespoons of chopped fresh parsley can be substituted for the scallions in this recipe. The peas or beans are cooked first in the milk and can then be simply added to the mashed potatoes or mashed with the potatoes.

Colcannon

For a dish that is not widely eaten or served today, colcannon remains remarkably widely known. Maybe the song about colcannon is better known than the dish. If you say "colcannon" in a crowded room, the chances are that half the room will break into one version of the song and the other half into a completely different version. Like the recipe itself, there are two versions commonly known.

Did you ever eat colcannon
When 'twas made with yellow
  cream
And the kale and praties blended
Like the picture in a dream?

Did you ever take a forkful
And dip it in the lake
Of heather-flavoured butter
That your mother used to make?

Oh you did, yes you did!
So did he and so did I,
And the more I think about it
Sure, the more I want to cry.

Did you ever eat colcannon
When 'twas made with thickened
  cream
And the greens and scallions
  blended
Like the picture in a dream?

Did you ever scoop a hole on top
To hold the melting cake
Of clover-flavoured butter
Which your mother used to make?

Did you ever eat and eat, afraid
You'd let the ring go past,
And some old married sprissman
Would get it at the last?

God be with the happy times
When trouble we had not
And our mothers made colcannon
In the little three-legged pot.

Colcannon is so like *champ*, *cally*, *stampy* and *poundies* that it is difficult to understand how it ever came to have a different name. Yet, all over the country, *colcannon* is *colcannon* and known as nothing else. As in the two versions of the song it can be made with kale or with greens, meaning cabbage. Those reared on the version made with kale can never understand how the cabbage version can be considered *colcannon* and those in the other camp, I'm perfectly sure, are equally insistent that their method is the true one. Nor do I like the addition of scallions. I was reared without them and believe that they spoil the very individual taste of the kale. Others would maintain that they are an essential ingredient. *Colcannon* is eaten at Hallowe'en, when the kale crop is ready, and often had a ring put into it—a tradition taken over by barmbrack in most parts of Ireland today.

> 2-2½ lb potatoes (cooked, mashed)
> 1 cup cooked kale (finely chopped)
> 1 cup hot milk
> 3-4 chopped scallions (optional)
> butter

Strip the heads of kale away from the stems and shred them finely. Kale is a tough vegetable which needs to cook for 10-20 minutes depending upon its age. Cook as you would for any green vegetable in furiously boiling salted water until it is just tender. Strain it and refresh it with cold water. Drain it thoroughly and squeeze out any remaining water. Nowadays I put the kale into a food processor with the hot milk and blend them into a green soup which I then mix through the mashed potatoes. I then re-heat it in the oven until it is very hot. This produces a dish fit for St. Patrick's Day in greenness. It is perfectly acceptable just to mix the kale and milk into the potatoes without recourse to the food processor, but the resulting dish is just speckled green. Do not use the processor if you are making colcannon with cabbage instead of kale. Do not forget the coin and the curtain ring to amuse the children.

Boxty

Boxty is another potato dish for which there are several competing recipes and songs. The different versions use different ingredients and methods of cooking. It is even, dare I say it, called *stampy* in some places. The thing all of the recipes have in common is grated raw potatoes. This was the

Hallowe'en dish in the northern part of the country, and it was common to insert a ring into the dish. Some of the rhymes refer to men and to running away with them.

> *Boxty on the griddle,*
> *Boxty in the pan*
> *If you don't eat your boxty*
> *You'll never get a man.*

Some girls obviously thought that neither the boxty nor the local men were worth having because the answering rhyme went:

> *I'll have none of your boxty,*
> *I'll have none of your blarney;*
> *But I'll whirl my petticoats over my head*
> *And be off with my Royal Charlie.*

Boxty has made something of a comeback recently. It is being produced commercially in County Mayo and sold ready-cooked and deep-frozen. In Dublin there is even a boxty restaurant serving the basic boxty with all kinds of untraditional toppings. Boxty as a dish is particularly associated with counties Cavan, Leitrim and parts of Monaghan.

Boxty Bread (Boxty On The Griddle)

    1-1¼ lb of raw peeled potatoes
    1-1¼ lb freshly cooked mashed potatoes
    4 oz flour
    salt

Grate the peeled raw potato into a clean cloth. Place the cloth over a bowl and twist the ends in order to wring out a starchy liquid from the potatoes which is caught in the bowl. Place the wrung, grated potato in another bowl and cover it with the cooked mashed potatoes. This prevents the grated potatoes from blackening. Allow the liquid from the potatoes to settle. The starch will drop to the bottom of the bowl. Pour off the clear liquid above the white starch and mix the starch into the potatoes in the other bowl. Mix them thoroughly. Now add the sifted flour and the salt and knead the potatoes as if you were kneading bread dough. Roll the dough out onto a floured top and cut it into farls (triangles), squares or circles. Bake these on a griddle or cook them in a heavy-bottomed pan. Cook them slowly until they are brown on one side. Turn them and cook them on the other side. The thickness of these boxty breads varies a lot. Long ago it would have been sliced in two and fried the next day for breakfast with the bacon. In my experience it was always made thinner than this and eaten fresh from the griddle. Both versions work.

Boxty Bread In The Oven

9 oz grated raw potatoes and their starch
9 oz cooked mashed potato
9 oz plain white flour
½ tsp baking powder
2-3 tbsp melted bacon fat
salt

Make this exactly as you would make griddle boxty but add the bacon fat (or butter). You may, or may not, need to add a little buttermilk, or milk, to the mixture to get a firm dough. Divide it into two pieces, roll them out and divide into farls. Bake in a pre-heated oven at 180°C (350°F, Gas Mark 4) for 35-40 minutes. Eat hot, split and buttered.

Boxty In The Pan

9 oz grated raw potatoes and their starch
9 oz freshly cooked, mashed potatoes
9 oz plain white or finely ground wholemeal flour
1-2 cups buttermilk
½ tsp bicarbonate of soda

This mixture makes a potato pancake. Combine the potatoes and the flour with the bicarbonate of soda. Add sufficient buttermilk to make a thick batter. Heat the pan until it is quite hot and proceed as for pancakes. Eat them hot, if possible straight from the pan, with butter, honey or sugar.

Potato Cakes

These are not sweet cakes but are more like plain soda cake. There are several regional variations of this recipe and the name will vary from place to place. *Fadge* or *tatie scones* are northern names. They are usually cooked in rounds and divided into triangular farls but, just to confuse people, when they are sold in shops these triangles are often called tatie "squares."

The only real difference between the recipes is the proportion of flour to cooked, mashed potato. Like most things Irish, it's a question of taste—the more potato, the softer (and moister) the cake. The commercial brands sold all over Ireland have a high proportion of flour, making them firmer and easier to handle and giving them a slightly longer shelf-life.

1 lb cooked, mashed floury potato
4-6 oz plain flour
¼ cup milk
2 tbsp melted bacon fat or butter

Mix all the ingredients except two tablespoonsful of the flour together in a bowl. Add just enough milk to get a firm dough. Sprinkle the remaining flour onto a flat work surface and roll out the dough into shapes roughly the size of a saucer, no more than half an inch thick. Cook them on a lightly greased griddle or heavy-bottomed pan until browned on both sides. This will take about 3 minutes on each side. They freeze well and can be re-heated in the oven, under the grill, but best of all fried in bacon fat.

Potato Soups

Potatoes are used as a base and thickening agent for a wide range of soups as well as for a classic plain potato soup. Our family favourite is a soup made from young nettle-tops picked in spring and early summer. I make it on a base of turkey stock where possible, although it works perfectly well with chicken stock or a good vegetable stock.

Nettle Soup

2 cups peeled diced potatoes
1 cup peeled chopped onion
3 cups washed young nettle-tops
5 cups turkey or chicken stock
2 tbsp butter or bacon fat

Sweat the potatoes and onion in the fat for about 10 minutes. You might use duck or goose fat instead of butter or bacon fat. The onion should be translucent. Add the stock and season with salt and freshly ground black pepper. Bring the stock to the boil then turn down the heat and simmer for 10 minutes. Add the nettles and simmer them for 5 minutes. Test them for tenderness. (They do not sting in any way once they are cooked.) Pass the soup through a mouli-sieve or use a food processor. Return the soup to the pan and re-heat. Serve with a spoonful of cream swirled into each bowl. Garnish with some fresh, chopped parsley or chives.

Watercress Soup

Watercress has always been an Irish favourite, as a salad, as a garnish and in sauces and soups. Before the introduction of cultivated cabbage (in the 16th century) it was served with bacon as a vegetable. It is found wild but is also cultivated commercially. You must be careful where you gather the wild cress. Never pick it downstream from cattle or sheep because of the danger of liver fluke. But even where these animals are present, as long as you refrain from eating it raw, and wash it thoroughly and boil it, it is safe enough. It is possible to grow and use land cress, or American cress as it is sometimes known, but this is rather bitter and peppery. When picking both wild watercress and the garden cress use a scissors rather than uprooting the plant.

> 2 cups peeled diced potatoes
> 1 cup chopped onion (optional)
> 6 cups chopped watercress
> a little cream
> 5 cups poultry stock (or milk and water mixed)
> cubes of crisped bacon (optional)

The method is identical to that for nettle soup. Be careful when seasoning this soup as watercress can be quite peppery in flavour. The onions should be sweated with the potatoes if you are adding them. I do. The garnish of crisped bacon is optional but I like it.

Potato Soup

> 3 cups peeled diced potatoes
> 3 cups chopped leeks (white and green)
> 1 stick celery (finely chopped)
> 5 cups good stock
> 1 oz butter or 2 tbsp bacon fat

Clean the leeks thoroughly to remove earth and grit, before chopping both the white stem and the green leaves. Sweat the vegetables in the fat until they are soft. Add the stock and bring it swiftly to the boil. Turn down the heat immediately and simmer gently for 20 minutes. Adjust the seasoning. This soup can be served as a vegetable broth or puréed. Serve with cream and small crisp croutons of bread fried in bacon fat.

An almost endless variety of soups can be made using this basic method. If you prefer to prevent the potatoes overwhelming the other vegetables, start out with a cup of diced potatoes and a cup of chopped onions to something between two and five cups of the main vegetable. If you vary the stock and the quantities of the main vegetable in proportion to the potato, then you will arrive, by experiment, at a method which is to your own taste. Do try to use good homemade stock since even the best commercial stock cubes tend to make all the soups taste the same.

Potato Pastries

Pratie Apples (Potato Apple Cake)

Originally cooked on a griddle over an open fire, these unusual little pasties can be successfully cooked in the oven. In some parts of the country these were a Hallowe'en treat and would have the traditional ring inserted into one of the cakes.

    1-1¼ lb hot mashed potato
    9 oz plain white flour
    ½ oz butter (melted)
    ½ tsp baking powder
    4 large cooking apples (peeled, cored and sliced)
    honey or brown sugar and butter to taste

Add the tablespoon of melted butter, the flour and baking powder (sifted) to the freshly cooked (still hot) mashed potatoes. Knead it lightly to get a soft dough and divide it into two equal pieces. Roll out one of these on a floured board until it is about half an inch thick. Divide it into four pointed farls. Place half of the thinly sliced apple on two of the farls. Place the other two farls on top and pinch the edges together well. Repeat this operation with the other piece of dough. You now have four pratie cakes. Cook on a medium heat griddle or pan until brown on the bottom. Turn them carefully and brown the second side.

Now you must carefully undo the good work you did pinching the edges of the cakes together. Carefully slit each cake lengthways and add thin slices of butter and brown sugar or honey over the apple. Replace the tops and continue cooking until the sweets have melted into a delicious sauce. I find it easier to cut a cross into the top pastry, open it out slightly, and spoon the butter/sugar mixture into the hole. If you are cooking them in the oven they will need about 15 minutes cooking until browned and another 5 after you have added the butter and sugar.

Potato Stuffing for Goose, Duck And Bodices

There is a strong tradition of using potato to stuff the cavities of all types of roast fowl, but particularly goose and duck, which release a lot of rich, delicious fat during cooking. Plain mashed potato with onion would be the commonest mixture, particu-larly with Cork Bodices, but there are a number of variations. In our household, the favourite is a potato, onion, herb and sausage-meat mixture—even with goose. The chosen herb varies with the meat: chopped sage leaves with pork; winter savoury, lemon balm, and thyme with goose or duck.

2-3 lb cooked mashed potatoes
1 lb onions (peeled, chopped)
½-¾ lb sausage-meat (optional)
1-2 tbsp chopped fresh herbs
1 tbsp chopped bacon fat or butter
1-2 cooking apples (peeled, cored, chopped) (optional)

The amounts are clearly going to be dictated by the size of the bird and can only be estimated by eye. If you make too much stuffing to fit in the bird's cavities then cook the remainder in a greased baking dish in the oven with the bird. It will need only an hour's cooking.

Melt the bacon fat or butter in a pan and soften the onions and apple chunks in it. (The apples are optional but are a traditional stuffing for goose.) If you are using sausage-meat, it should be browned, broken up and cooked through in the pan before being added to the mixture. Mix all the ingredients together in a large bowl and season the mixture well with salt and freshly ground black pepper. Use as required.

Potato Pastry

A delicious shortcrust pastry can be made by substituting cooked potatoes for a proportion of the flour. The amount of potato varies from recipe to recipe and each Irish cook will swear by their own particular mixture. The first version I give is very rich indeed and heavier on fat than most people today would consider necessary. It does, however, produce a light crust which can be used for topping fruit or savoury pies, or used as a base for small savoury tarts.

3 oz self-raising flour
3 oz cooked mashed potatoes
6 oz butter
pinch of salt

Rub the butter into the flour with your fingers and when it is like breadcrumbs mix in the potatoes as lightly as you can. Knead lightly and roll out as if it was an ordinary shortcrust pastry.

The second recipe uses less butter but uses an egg to bind and enrich the pastry. Throwing in an egg in this way is a particularly Irish habit, certainly in farmhouses where the woman of the house kept hens.

      4 oz self-raising flour
      4 oz cooked mashed potatoes
      3 oz butter
      1 beaten egg
      pinch of salt

Proceed exactly as in the last recipe but add the egg at the last. This makes a rather less delicate pastry than the first but is easier to handle.

CHAPTER SIX
THE CUP THAT CHEERS

By 1880, thirty years after the Great Famine, 5 million acres, or about one-quarter of the land surface of Ireland, had changed ownership. Gone, except from the west of Ireland, were the cottier class who existed on small plots of land; gone too were many of the landlords, whose bankrupt estates changed hands under the Encumbered Estates Act. Over a period of fifty years, with the help of piecemeal legislation forced by political unrest, the transfer of land to farmers, both large and small, was complete. Continuing emigration during the same half-century brought down the population to half of what it had been before the famines.

On some of the poorest land in the country, all along the western seaboard, the population continued to grow. The West has always gone its own sweet way. In earlier times it had clung to the Gaelic way of life; now it clung to a way of life dominated by seasonal emigration, to work in Scotland and the North of England, in order to supplement the small patch of land, often no bigger than a garden, at home. The Congested Districts Board was set up towards the end of the century with the aim of improving husbandry (of the land), fishing, and to encourage industry in the west of Ireland.

I remember my childish incredulity when, staring out of the window of a moving car in County Donegal at the ruined cottages, the treeless, barren countryside, I was informed that the area was known as a congested district. It was a well-meant initiative but it was something of a joke as well. No one got more mileage out of the joke than that much underrated novelist George A. Birmingham. Birmingham was the pseudonym of a Church of Ireland rector of Westport, Canon James

Owen Hannay, who, in a series of novels and stories, pilloried the building, by the Congested Districts Board, of tiny little piers all along the western coast. Today their efforts can be appreciated by tourists and holiday-makers, but at the time they did little to alleviate the poverty in these areas where, as L.M. Cullen has pointed out, there were only two classes of people—the poor and the destitute. Of far greater use was the money sent home by the emigrants who, from the turn of the century right up to the present day, have left to better themselves both within Ireland and abroad.

They fled from the land to the cities in search of the work that no longer existed in the countryside. In the fifty years following the Great Famine the population of the cities and towns, mainly Dublin, Belfast and Derry, rose from one-eighth of the population of the country to over a third. Today Greater Dublin alone holds 35 per cent of the population of the Republic.

At the turn of the century they were drawn to Belfast by the growing linen and ship-building industries and to Dublin by the brewing and distilling industries which were characterised by the scale of their operations. Guinness's Dublin brewery was the largest in the British Isles. Brewing and distilling provided work for many tradesmen as well as labourers: brewers, clerks, coopers, grain merchants, timber merchants, seamen and building craftsmen.

It should never be forgotten that Dublin was long considered the second city of the Empire. It was a cultured, attractive, elegant capital city long before Birmingham, Liverpool or Manchester came to commercial prominence. Life in Dublin in the mid-19th century must have been very pleasant if you belonged to the upper class, who lived in the outer sub-urbs, or to the merchant or professional middle-classes living round private enclosed squares like Fitzwilliam, Merrion or St. Stephen's Green. Here were elegant hotels, The Mansion House Supper Rooms, The Rotunda Concert Rooms. Here street-hawkers sold everything from oysters, at half a crown per hundred, to muffins, honey, strawberries and lavender. On Fridays the ladies taking their solitary, constitutional walks within the locked gates of Merrion Square would hear the fishman selling Dublin Bay herrings. A hundred years later I took my play as a child in the same private square, letting myself into this teeming wilderness within a city with the same large iron key they must have used.

But the poor people who flooded into the city lived a very different life, just a stone's throw away in places like the Liberties. Three-quarters of the population of Dublin lived in one-room tenements housing, on average, six people to a small room. Not for them the dinners of goose, beef, veal, turkey, venison, partridge, quail, rabbit, crab or pickled salmon; not for them onions, endive, orange butter, cherries and Dutch cheese. If they were lucky, when they arrived just after the Famine, they might have supped on the famous famine soup devised by Alexis Soyer, chef of the great Reform Club in London. He used a 300-gallon boiler into which he put ox heads (without the tongues), maize, carrots, turnips, cabbages, onions, peas and leeks. I imagine the nourish-ment from this soup was very much related to the amount of water he added.

The diet of the very poor in the second half of the 19th century was black tea and bread with, for those who could afford it, the addition of herrings, dripping, and the occasional pig's cheek. And yet, as in Cobbett's day, right alongside this abject poverty, the manufacture and distribution of food and drink was big business. At the turn of the century there were 30 cattle-dealers who exported 15,000 cattle, sheep, pigs (and the odd goat) each week. There were 600 dairies supplying milk to the capital. A Frenchwoman, Madame de Bovet, described the permanent market street of St. Patrick's thus: "shops with overhanging roofs expose for sale sides of rancid bacon, jars of treacle, greens, cauliflowers, and musty turnips, flat baskets are spread with cows' feet, overkept sheeps' heads, flabby pink veal, skins and fat of every animal, and at every three doors a tavern."

The Irish have been brewing and distilling since the earliest times. I have no doubt that had the climate been suitable we would have developed a thriving wine industry. Not that we did without wine. Wine has been imported into Ireland since the Celts arrived. Contemporary records from Bordeaux show that they were exporting wine to Ireland two thousand years ago for "Feasts in the courts of the kings." The early Christian monks braved pirates to sail to the mouth of the Loire to fetch wine for the Irish monasteries and we have already noticed that the Vikings paid tribute to Brian Boru with vats of wine.

While kings and monks drank wine, the ordinary people were happy with their home-brewed ale and cider. Brewed from barley and some other grains and flavoured with hops which grew wild, the Irish developed beers quite different to those of most of Europe. Our three great beers were ale, porter and stout. For the technically minded all three were "top fermented." Ale is light in colour with a pronounced taste of hops and has a tartness which sets it apart from other beers. Porter is no longer brewed but was dark brown with a slightly sweet, malty flavour. Stout is very dark with a distinctive, rich, malt flavour and a bitter taste of hops.

In the ancient literature there are many descriptions of large quantities of ale being drunk at banquets and voices being raised in song as a result. At one such feast in Ulster 100 barrels were consumed and the sound of the singing is said to have disturbed the peace of Munster. Anyone could brew ale for his own use, but the Brehon Laws regulated ale-houses. Ale was drunk both cold, or hot and flavoured with spice.

The larger breweries were started by the monasteries and supplied not only the monks but the surrounding countryside. Even the saints brewed—St. Patrick had his own brewer, but St. Brigid did it herself. Mead, which is the school history drink of heroes, was made from honey and was, therefore, always a rare delicacy.

When the secret art of distillation was brought to Ireland from the Mediterranean, some fifteen hundred years ago, we developed a distilled drink, *uisce beatha*—the water of life. Our missionary monks brought the recipe with them to Scotland where it became known as *uiscebaugh* and was the drink which eventually developed into whisky as we know it today. When the Normans came to Ireland they liked *uisce* a lot and they anglicised the word to whiskey. The first mention of whiskey in literature is the tale of a man who drank so much of the water of life that, for him, it became the "water of death."

Within The Pale of Dublin, where the Normans held sway, they introduced regulations to control brewing—women had a monopoly of the industry (although only men were allowed to sell wine and meat). These hardy, liberated women introduced the earliest form of "pub grub" (bar food) when they served oysters and salmon along with their ale, and, it must be admitted, their services as whores. Beside the priory of Christchurch, within the "Liberties," was a network of streets whose names, even today, proclaim their connections with food and drink: Sheep Street, Fishamble Street, Fleshamble Street, Skinners' Row. Down towards the river and Merchant's Quay, just across the river, we find Fishers Lane, Commarket, and Oxmantown Road. Cook Street, near Christchurch Cathedral, was where the Guild of Cooks set up an early form of take-away when they supplied to the priory delicacies known as *coffins*—a tasty pie made from larks. Close at hand was Winetavern Street where, after the Reformation, the Elizabethans professed themselves shocked by the number of drinking-houses: "The whole profit of the town stands upon ale-houses, taverns are open day and night and every minute of the hour. Every filthy ale-house is thronged full of company."

This love of drink was in no way confined to the city. An Englishman writing a "discourse on Ireland" explained the drinking customs in country houses. As soon as he entered he was offered "first ordinary beer, then *uisce beatha*, then sack, then old ale." He pointed out that "you must not refuse it and you may drink a noggin without offence." On leaving he was offered again all the different drinks of the house and given, finally, a "dogh a dores." Roughly translated this means a drink at the door. This whole passage is remarkably similar to country hospitality today. When you arrive you will be pressed to "take a little something". You will, and it will turn out to be quite a bit of something. Then, before you finally get out of the door, you'll be encouraged to have "one for the road."

It is clear that, as late as the 17th century, flavourings were often added to the whiskey: raisins, fennel seeds, even liquorice.

Today, at home, people still flavour gin and vodka with sloes. With the setting up of industrial distilleries (the oldest surviving one is the Bushmill's Distillery near Coleraine, opened in 1608), whiskey became a standardised product made only from barley, malted and unmalted, yeast and pure water. It was distilled three times, matured in oak barrels for between five and twelve years, and became famous all over the world.

Charles II, after the Restoration of the monarchy in Britain, was the first to see the potential of taxing drink in Ireland. His new tax, of four pence on every gallon, may not seem much today when the major part of the cost of each bottle goes to the exchequer, but it forced the Irish to take up home-distilling in a big way once more. It also ushered in the great days of smuggling, mainly brandy, from Europe. There were other incentives to encourage local distilling enterprises. A farmer often found it easier and more profitable, even when the price he might get for his barley was good, to transport the much smaller cargo of distilled *poitín,* as the illegal distillation was called. It became an underground industry supporting travelling craftsmen who built and repaired stills, carters and smugglers who distributed the liquor, informers who ferreted out the sites of the illicit stills for the authorities, droves of excisemen (backed up by the military) who enforced the law. One barony in County Donegal was reputed to support 800 illicit stills. Even so, the demand for whiskey in 1779 was enough to support one thousand legal distilleries.

Breweries abounded (Arthur Guinness opened his first brewery in Dublin in 1759) and Irish merchants were firmly established in Bordeaux. Some Irish families, descendants of The Wild Geese, had established vineyards in France and today, still proudly bearing their Irish names, they are numbered among the distinguished names of the French wine trade: Hennessey, Palmer, Barton, Lynch, Sullivan, O'Brien, McCarthy. Many acquired titles and châteaux from the wealth they accumulated dealing in drink.

Complicated regulations, based on the size and capacity of the still, for calculating the tax due on spirits put three-quarters of the distilleries out of business in a ten-year period and cleared the way for the big distilleries to become, along with the breweries, the first major industries in Ireland. *Poitín*-making declined too, but it has never completely died out in the west and south of the country despite the best efforts of the authorities.

Beverage Recipes

Irish Cream Liqueur Granita (Water Ice)

Bailey's Irish Cream was the first Irish cream liqueur, made of whiskey and cream, to be marketed but, since 1975, it has been followed by several other brands. They are a popular drink and can be used successfully in cooking.

    1½ lb sugar
    10 cups water
    2½ cups Irish cream liqueur

Make a syrup of the sugar in the water and let it cool. Stir in the cream liqueur. Now pour the mixture into a shallow container and place it in the ice-box of your refrigerator. Leave it until the syrup has become icy at the edges. Whisk the whole mixture to distribute and break up the crystals of ice. Replace in the ice-box. Repeat this process at least twice more. This is necessary to prevent large ice crystals forming. Serve this delicious pudding in a glass or a bowl decorated with borage leaves and a borage flower. Do not attempt to store it for more than a day or so because the lovely whiskey flavour and aroma will be lost.

Irish Mist Soufflé

Irish Mist was the first widely marketed Irish liqueur and is based upon a long-lost recipe from the past. The story goes that an Austrian refugee ended up in Tullamore Town, long a bastion of Irish whiskey-distilling, clutching "an old Irish recipe" that had been in his family for a very long time. Irish Mist is based on that recipe. True or not, the result is a very distinctive liqueur.

  3 oz butter
  2 oz flour
  1¼ cups milk
  2 oz caster sugar
  4 large eggs (separated)
  2 tbsp Irish Mist Liqueur

Beat the egg whites until stiff, adding the sugar, as if you were making meringues. Make a roux with the butter and flour, stirring over a gentle heat for 2 minutes. Add in the milk and stir to mix it through. Cook gently for 5 minutes. Add the Irish Mist Liqueur. Allow to cool slightly then beat in the egg yolks, one at a time. Stir in 1 tablespoon of the stiffly beaten egg whites then fold in the remainder. Turn out gently into a two-pint soufflé dish. Bake at once for 40-45 minutes in a pre-heated oven at 190°C (375°F, Gas Mark 5). Serve with a sauce made from raspberries, blackberries or fraughans.

The raspberries will need no sweetening. To prepare the sauce, just pass the fruit through a mouli-sieve to remove the seeds. Blackberries (black currants) and fraughans (whortle-berries) will need roughly ¼ lb of sugar for each 1lb of fruit. Simply stew the fruit and the sugar together, gently, until the fruit is soft, and then work the mixture through the mouli-sieve to remove the skins and seed. These sauces can all be prepared in advance and re-heated to serve with the soufflé.

Mulled Ale

> 2 beaten eggs
> 2½ cups ale
> 3 tsp honey or sugar
> 1 tbsp melted butter
> ¼ tsp ground nutmeg, cinnamon or cloves

To be perfectly honest I have included this recipe simply because it was what people used to do to ale. I do not like it but others might.

Beat the eggs in a bowl with one tablespoon of the ale until they are frothy. Heat the rest of the ale in a pot until very hot but not boiling. Pour the hot ale over the eggs whisking all the time as you do so. Return the mixture to the pot and add the honey or sugar (to taste), the butter and the spice. Heat it up again but do not let it boil. Drink hot.

Hot Whiskey Punch

> 1 measure of Irish whiskey
> 1 slice lemon
> 3-4 whole cloves
> sugar or honey to taste

Heat a glass by placing a metal teaspoon into it and filling the glass with nearly boiling water. The spoon absorbs heat more quickly than the glass and so prevents the glass cracking. Assemble all the other ingredients. Empty the glass and add the whiskey, lemon, cloves and sugar to it. Give it a quick stir and press the lemon slice to release some juice. Now add nearly boiling water to almost fill the glass.

The instruction to drink this while hot is superfluous, as a feature of this wonderful drink is the speed with which it disappears and has to be replaced by another and another . . .

Scáiltín

Sometimes called a milk punch, there were several ways of making it. Made cold, by simply mixing a measure of milk with a measure of whiskey, it was known as a *sandwich*—so be careful if you walk into an old shebeen looking for a sandwich at lunch-time. In my youth (my father ran a bar) it was, I think, a rough-and-ready way of recreating the old *scáiltín* which was a method, I suspect, used exclusively to "take the harm out" of *poitín* of doubtful quality. The milk was supposed to line the stomach. Butter, sugar and a good pinch of ground cinnamon or cloves were often added. The method is the same as for hot whiskey and it is perfectly reasonable to substitute whiskey for the *real stuff*.

Posset Cup

I think these have completely died out now and, to be honest, I'm not altogether surprised. They are a sort of curdled milk, oatmeal and ale drink, but wine, or whiskey, was often substituted for the ale.

> 2½ cups milk or water
> 2 tbsp oatmeal (flaked)
> pinch of salt
> 2 tsp honey
> 2½ cups ale or stout
> ½ tsp ground cinnamon or nutmeg

Put the milk in a pot with the oatmeal and salt. Stir it while heating it almost to boiling-point. Remove it from the heat and allow it to stand for about 10 minutes. Strain the liquid into a fresh pot and add the ale, honey and spice. Heat them together and drink hot.

Sloe Gin

The tradition of adding herbs, spices, or berries to whiskey and *poitín* has all but died out. The last time I drank *poitín* which had been flavoured in this way was over twenty years ago and a fine, dark, rich colour and flavour it had. But this gin liqueur is popular and simplicity itself to prepare. You'll have to find your sloes (the fruit of the blackthorn bush) and buy the gin.

½ lb sloe berries
2 tbsp sugar (or less to taste)
8 almonds (blanched and cracked)
¾ bottle gin

Pick the sloes in October, preferably after they've had a touch of autumn frost. Remove all the stems and wash the berries. Now prick them all over with a fork. Drop each berry, as you do this, into an empty bottle. There is a school of thought which maintains that you need 2 bottles of gin to make this recipe—1¼ bottles of gin to be drunk in order to get the empty bottle. The berries will almost come up to the top of the bottle by the time you have them all in. Add the sugar and the blanched and cracked almonds. It is possible to take some stones from sloes and crack them with a hammer. These are substituted for the almonds. Carefully pour gin into the bottle over the berries and almonds. Cap the bottle tightly. It is usual to shake the contents of the bottle once a week for about 3 months and then allow it to stand undisturbed for a further 6 months. Now strain the liqueur into a clean bottle and store it in a dark place until ready to drink during the second Christmas. It is wonderful if you can restrain yourself that long.

Irish Coffee

This is probably the best-known Irish whiskey drink in the minds of tourists. The Irish are pretty fond of it themselves. Joe Sheridan, once the chef at the flying-boat base at Foynes, Co. Clare (near Shannon), was its creator, despite the fact that Shannon Airport usually gets the credit.

> 1 measure Irish whiskey
> 1 measure strong black coffee
> 2 tsp sugar
> 1-2 tbsp fresh double (thick)cream

Heat the glass. Pour in the whiskey, add the sugar and the hot coffee. Pour the lightly whipped cream gently onto the top of the mixture over the back of a teaspoon. Experts use unwhipped cream and consider whipping the sign of an unsteady hand or a coward! It should float on top. You cannot make this without the sugar as it is the sugar in solution which allows the cream to float. It is drunk through the cream.

CHAPTER SEVEN
A NEW TRADITION

It is difficult to pin down exactly why, as a people, we lost touch with our historic traditions in the preparation and cooking of our food. Certainly, in the first half of the 20th century, one had to search hard to find evidence of that tradition in public eating places.

Honor Moore maintains, and I share her belief, that the suppression of the old Gaelic civilisation had much to do with it. Any schooling the common people received was through Irish and Latin and the brutal suppression of the Gaelic language meant that, with an inevitable increase in illiteracy, much of the written tradition, recipes and methods, must have died with the language. It must be equally true that after the famines, much of the daily effort of ordinary people went into simply managing to eat, with a consequent disregard for how food was being prepared or cooked. Simple poverty, the lack of basic amenities and utensils, dictated that food was cooked all in the one pot. Hard upon this came the growing struggle for independence from Britain and the decline in the great house tradition in the country. As these houses declined in number, through the defection of their owners, another training ground for many young women in the arts of the kitchen was cut off. Two world wars followed hard upon the gaining of independence and it was not until the fifties of this century that the modern Irish State began to emerge.

During this period, and between the wars, most of the training was inevitably aimed at home economics and, where training in cooking skills was offered, it was aimed at filling an urgent need for institutional catering, for schools and hospitals. While the training was undoubtably sound it paid little heed to what was intrinsically Irish. The gap for skilled chefs in the hotel and restaurant world had been filled, in the thirties, forties and fifties, by foreign-trained chefs, most of whom were trained in the tradition of French *haute cuisine*. The first new generation of Irish restaurateurs and chefs learned their skills under them and others trained abroad. It was not until the sixties and seventies that a renewed interest in what was best in the Irish tradition began to be noticeable once more.

Ireland is still predominantly an agricultural country—we produce far more than we can eat or drink ourselves—and our trading surplus with the world is based on the export of food-stuffs. Much of what we export we have been exporting since the earliest times. Our high-quality grasslands still produce prime beef and dairy produce. Our lambs, which graze the mountain pastures, are much sought after in Europe, as is the harvest of our seas, rivers and lakes. There is a thriving and increasingly respected farmhouse cheese industry and a growing organic farming movement. Just lately there has been a serious recognition by government and people alike that our country-side is our greatest asset and that we harm it at our peril.

A growing tourist trade, especially with our European neighbours, has encouraged us to look again at how we cater for visitors and has brought to prominence a band of exciting young chefs and restaurateurs who are no longer content to ape the dishes of French *haute cuisine*. Following the lead of the indomitable Myrtle Allen and the Ryan Brothers in Cork, they are looking afresh at our own food traditions.

The recipes which follow are a selection from this new tradition, dishes based on traditional foodstuffs, conceived and served in a specifically Irish context to the highest possible standard.

Ballymaloe House, near Cloyne in Co. Cork, is an early 18th-century house with the remains of a much earlier Geraldine castle attached to one of its wings. It stands in its own grounds not far from the sea at Ballycotton. Since 1947 it has been the family home of Ivan and Myrtle Allen who, when their family were grown, turned the house first into a restaurant, the famous Yeats Room, and gradually into a comfortable, friendly and deservedly popular guest-house.

The Allens were farmers and market gardeners before they became restaurateurs and at Ballymaloe, as far as is humanly possible, everything from herbs and vegetables to fowl and pigs, is grown on the estate. Fish comes fresh from the sea at Ballycotton. Myrtle Allen is a splendid cook and has spearheaded the return to a recognisably Irish cooking tradition. Her daughter-in-law Darina continues the tradition in her cookery school nearby.

Ballymaloe Dressed Crab

(Serves 5-6 main course helpings)

    3 cups crab meat
    1½ cups breadcrumbs
    ½ tbsp white vinegar
    2 tbsp chutney
    1 oz butter
    generous pinch of dry mustard powder
        or 1 level tsp French mustard
    salt and pepper
    ½ cup white sauce
     cup buttered crumbs

Mix all the ingredients together. Taste for seasoning. Pack into clean, scrubbed crab shells or into ramekins. Top with buttered breadcrumbs. Bake in a moderately hot oven until heated through and brown on top, 20 minutes at 200°C (400°F, Gas Mark 6).

Note: 1 lb cooked crab, in the shell, yields 4-6 oz approximately of crab meat.

Ballymaloe Dingle Pie

Myrtle Allen writes:

Pies were made for special occasions in Dingle (Co. Kerry), for Lady Day in September, Holy Thursday and November's Day (All Saints). They were made for fair-days when nobody had time to sit down to a proper meal but the pie shops flourished and the children chattered with delight:

> *Make a pie, make a pie, make a pie.*
> *Roll a pie, roll a pie, roll a pie.*
> *Pinch a pie, pinch a pie, pinch a pie.*

For the farmers and fishermen they provided a sustaining snack. They were made from scraps of mutton or the meat of a sheep's head, for Dingle is in mountainous sheep country. It is a sheltered meeting place before that wild peninsula plunges into the great Atlantic.

There were several recipes for mutton pies in and about Dingle. All are very simple. The pastry was shortened with butter, dripping or mutton fat, sometimes moistened with hot milk. It was rolled out and cut with a saucer. The meat was seasoned and heaped in the middle and a smaller circle of pastry, cut with a tumbler, was placed on top. The pastry base was brought up to fit over the top circle, pleated to fit, the edges moistened and pinched on. They were baked in a slow to moderate oven for about an hour, or boiled in a stock made out of the mutton bones. Fishermen brought them to sea in a can and heated them up in the stock over a little fire made in a tin box, at the bottom of the boat. A cold baked pie was better for the farmer's pocket.

The spiced mutton pies described here are not Dingle Pies, but were inspired by them—a more sophisticated descendant. The pastry is a rich hot-water crust, made with a lot of butter. Serve hot or cold. Good for picnics.

For two pies (6" x 1½") to serve 6-8 helpings.

for the filling:
1 lb boneless mutton
2¼ cups onions
1¾ cups carrots
1 tsp cumin seed
1¼ cups stock
2 tbsp flour
salt and pepper

for the piecrust:
3½ cups flour
1¼ cups butter (approx.)
¾ cup water
pinch of salt

Put bones and vegetable trimmings in cold water and simmer to make a stock, if none is already available. Cut surplus fat away from the meat. Chop it finely and render it down in a heavy pot over medium heat. Cut the remaining meat into small neat pieces about the size of sugar lumps. Cut the vegetables into slightly smaller dice and toss them in the fat in the bottom of the pot, leaving them to cook for 3-4 minutes. Remove the vegetables and toss the meat in remaining fat until the colour turns. Stir in flour and spice. Cook gently for 2 minutes and blend in the stock gradually. Bring to the boil, stirring occasionally. Add the vegetables and leave to simmer in a covered pot. If using young lamb, 30 minutes will be sufficient, an older animal can take up to 2 hours. Meanwhile make pastry cases.

Sieve flour and salt into a mixing bowl, and make a well in the middle. Put butter and water into a saucepan and bring to the boil. Pour the liquid all at once into the flour and mix together quickly; beat until smooth. At first the pastry will be too soft to handle, but as it cools it can be rolled out 5mm (¹/₈ - ¼ inch) thick to fit into two tins 6 inches in diameter and 1½ inches high. It can also be made into individual pies as described above. Keep back one-third of the pastry for lids. Fill up the cases with the meat mixture which should be almost, but not quite, cooked and cooled a little. Moisten the pastry at the top of the pies and place the lids on, pinching them tightly together. Cut a slit in the lid, brush with egg wash. Bake the pies for 40 minutes approximately at 190°C (375°F, Gas Mark 5). They can be eaten hot or cold and are good for picnics.

Ballymaloe Carrageen Moss Pudding with Irish Coffee or Caramel Sauce

Serves 4 - 6

for the pudding:
½ cup cleaned, well-dried carrageen
   (1 semi-closed fistful)
3¾ cups milk
2 tbsp sugar
1 egg
½ tsp vanilla essence or 1 vanilla pod

for the Irish Coffee sauce:
1 cup sugar
⅓ cup water
1 cup coffee
1 tbsp Irish whiskey

for the caramel sauce:
1 cup sugar
1⅓ cups hot water

Soak the carrageen in tepid water for 10 minutes. Put in a saucepan with milk and a vanilla pod if used. Bring to the boil and simmer very gently for 20 minutes. Pour through a strainer into a mixing bowl. The carrageen will now be swollen and exuding jelly. Rub all this jelly through the strainer and beat it into the milk with the sugar, egg yolk and vanilla essence, if used. Test for a set in a saucer as one would with gelatine. Whisk the egg white stiffly and fold it in gently. It will rise to make a fluffy top. Serve chilled with a fruit compote, caramel or Irish Coffee sauce.

To make a caramel, dissolve the sugar in ⅓-cup water over heat and continue cooking to a caramel. Remove from heat. Pour in 1 cup of water and continue cooking until caramel is dissolved and smooth. Do not stir.

To make the Irish Coffee sauce make a caramel as above. Add coffee (made to drinking strength) instead of water. Cool and add whiskey.

Arbutus Lodge Hotel, Montenotte, Cork City

The Arbutus Lodge Hotel, run by Declan and Michael Ryan, has been famous as a place to enjoy some of the finest food in Ireland for many years. From its lovely Victorian dining-room, you can look down from the hills of Montenotte on the city of Cork and the River Lee.

The brothers, whose fame (like Myrtle Allen's) reaches far beyond these shores, have consistently set the standard in Ireland for good food, based on the finest local ingredients, and offer a choice of menus including their famous Taster Menu. Lunch from 1-2 p.m., dinner from 7-9.30 p.m. Monday through Saturday. The wine cellar has been awarded the Egon Ronay/Armagnac Award for the best wine cellar in Britain and Ireland.

Arbutus Lodge Nettle Soup

    1 leek
    ¼ lb butter
    1 bunch (2 cups) young nettle-tops
    1 lb potatoes
    2 pints chicken stock
    ¼ pint cream
    salt and pepper

Clean and chop the whole leek and sweat it in the butter. Add the washed and chopped nettles and cook them until they appear glossy. Stir in the peeled and sliced potatoes and add the stock. Simmer the mixture for 30-35 minutes. Liquidise the soup, return it to the heat and add the cream, salt and pepper. Serve hot.

Arbutus Lodge Forester's Pie

Declan Ryan writes: This is a sophisticated version of traditional peasant fare. Serves 4.

    1 lb puff pastry
    ½ lb chicken breast (or lean veal)
    ½ lb pheasant, pigeon or venison
    1 lb potato (finely sliced)
    2 oz finely chopped shallots
    1 oz butter
    2 tbsp groundnut oil
    3 tbsp reduced cream
    chopped parsley, thyme and chives
    salt and pepper
    egg wash

All of the meat should be finely chopped and not minced. The finely sliced potatoes should be rinsed in cold water to remove the starch.

Sweat the shallots in a little butter. Mix all the ingredients except the cream and the eggwash. Roll out the puff pastry into two circles, with one slightly larger than the other. Place the mixture in the centre of the larger circle of pastry leaving a 1-inch lap round the edge. Eggwash this edge to stick the second round which is placed on top. Fold over the lower edge and seal with the back of a fork. Eggwash the top surface of the pie and score a design with a sharp knife. Cook for 45 minutes in a pre-heated medium oven at 190°C (375°F, Gas Mark 5) until the pie is golden. Cut a small circle in the top of the pie and add in the seasoned cream which has been reduced by boiling. Serve the pie on a bed of acidulated butter sauce (or beurre blanc).

Arbutus Lodge Chocolate Gâteau

for the sponge:
4 large eggs
4 oz caster sugar
8 oz cream flour
1 oz cocoa powder
1 oz butter (melted)

for the icing:
1 lb best chocolate
½ pint cream
sugar syrup laced with jamaica rum

Bake the sponge in a deep baking tray, either in one piece or in three equal-sized pieces. Whichever way you do this you will need three layers. Make a thin sugar syrup by boiling sugar with water. Lace the syrup with jamaica rum to taste. Moisten the sponge layers with the sugar syrup. Prepare the icing by melting the chocolate, adding the cream and boiling them up together. Work the icing when it has cooled. Layer the sponges with the icing between each layer and end with a final icing—use a hot palette knife to achieve the final gloss. Refrigerate before serving.

Michael Clifford, the chef-patron of Clifford's Restaurant, after initial training in Ireland, spent seven years in France and Holland (he still takes an annual busman's holiday on the Continent) before returning to be chef at White's On The Green in Dublin. While there Michael built up a fine reputation as a skilled and innovative chef. He moved to Cork, his home town, to open a small restaurant in Washington Street which proved so popular that recently he had to move to larger premises where he can also provide rooms for private parties. He changes his menus frequently and has a good wine list. Michael was recently elected a life-member of the prestigious World Master Chefs Society, one of only eight Irish master chefs so honoured.

Clifford's Warm Black Pudding Salad

> 1 apple
> 1 medium ring black pudding
> 2 tbsp vinaigrette dressing
> 1 tbsp sherry
> 1 tbsp white wine
> 1 oz butter
> black pepper and salt
> selection of salads

Michael Clifford specifies that the black pudding should come from Clonakilty in County Cork and I thoroughly agree with him. The puddings there, particularly from one very accomplished butcher, are coarse-textured and mealy with oats, quite different in flavour from the denser, more solid puddings which most butchers make. However, I would not deny yourself the pleasure of this splendid dish for the want of a trip to Clonakilty. Use your own favourite pudding. The apple should be cored but not peeled. Use a good dessert apple like a Cox's Pippin, a russet or a Worcester.

Slice the black pudding and the apple into rings. Place them in a hot pan with the butter and fry gently until golden brown. Set them aside. Arrange the salads in a round serving dish and toss with the vinaigrette dressing. Meanwhile add the wine and sherry to the pan in which the apple and the pudding were fried and bubble them up to make a glaze for the pudding. Arrange the pieces of black pudding, with the apple, on the salads and then pour the glaze over the black pudding pieces. Season with coarse sea salt and freshly ground black pepper.

Clifford's Gourmet Irish Stew
Serves 4

    1 shoulder of young lamb
    2 carrots (chopped)
    4 potatoes (chopped)
    1 onion (chopped)
    2 small white turnips (chopped)
    2 sticks celery (chopped)
    2 oz green cabbage (finely shredded)
    ¼ pint cream
    dash of Worcester sauce
    1 leek (finely sliced)
    chopped fresh parsley
    salt and freshly ground black pepper

Ask your butcher to bone the shoulder and to chop up the bones into small pieces. Cut the lamb into cubes and place in a large pot with the bones. Cover the meat with cold water and bring to the boil. Drain the meat and rinse it before putting it (and the bones) into a clean pot. Cover with 2 pints of water. Add the prepared vegetables but set aside 1 carrot, 1 turnip, 2 of the potatoes and the green cabbage for later use as a garnish. Cover the pot when it comes to the boil, turn down the heat and simmer gently for 1 hour, or until the meat is tender. Remove the meat and bones from the pot with a slotted spoon.

Discard the bones. Liquidise the cooked vegetables in their juice and return them to the pot. Add the cream, Worcester sauce and a handful of chopped parsley. Neatly chop and blanch the remaining potatoes, carrot and turnip. Return the meat and the blanched vegetables to the pot. Taste for seasoning.

Serve in warm deep plates with extra chopped parsley and freshly made wholemeal bread.

Drimcong House Restaurant, Moycullen, Co. Galway

Gerry and Mary Galvin run their elegant restaurant in a 300-year-old country manor house eight miles north of Galway City, on the Moycullen to Oughterard road. The delight-ful dining-room seats fifty and the moderately priced menu changes frequently. This is dictated by the availability of the finest produce and Gerry Galvin's own mood. Drimcong House Restaurant is considered to be one of the finest in Ireland, has a fine wine list and serves dinner between 7 p.m. and 10 p.m. from Tuesday through Saturday.

Drimcong Oyster Broth
Serves 4

> 1 pint fish stock
> ¼ pint cream
> 12 oysters
> 1 tbsp dry white wine
> 4 drops tabasco
> 1 tbsp chopped fresh fennel, or sweet cecily, or chervil

Bring the fish stock, cream, wine and herb to the boil and reduce briskly for 3 minutes. Open the oysters and remove the flesh from the shell. Liquidise all the ingredients and return to the pan. Bring quickly to the boil and serve at once.

Drimcong Steamed Brill in Carrot Sauce
Serves 4

4 (6 oz) fillets of brill
2 large carrots
1 oz finely chopped onion
2 small cloves garlic (crushed)
2 sprigs fresh thyme
1½ pints fish stock
salt, pepper and lemon juice

Peel and chop the carrots. Sweat the onion in a non-stick pan without fat, over a gentle heat, until it is soft but not brown. Add the crushed garlic and toss with the onion for 5 seconds. Put onion, garlic, carrots and thyme into the fish stock and bring it quickly to the boil. Cover and turn down the heat. Simmer for 15 minutes. Remove the thyme sprigs. Liq-uidise and taste. Season to taste with salt, pepper and lemon juice. Taste again. Sieve the sauce for a more refined finish and keep hot. Season the brill fillets and steam them for about 8 minutes, until cooked.

Present the steamed fish with pools of sauce for a simple and healthy dish.

Drimcong Apples in Red Wine
Serves 4

6 large apples
1 pint red wine
2 cloves
1 stick of cinnamon
4 oz sugar

Choose apples of a type which hold their shape in cooking, such as Granny Smiths or Golden Delicious. Bring the wine, cloves, sugar and cinnamon to the boil in a saucepan. Simmer for 5 minutes. Peel, core and segment the apples and immerse in the mulled wine. Bring the wine back to the boil and then allow to cool slightly before serving the apple pieces, dressed with a little of the mulled syrup on a plate with whipped fresh cream, vanilla ice-cream or cream cheese flavoured with honey and lemon.

This dessert can be stored in a jar and kept for a few days in the fridge before being quickly re-heated. It can also be served cold.

Jury's Hotel, Ballsbridge, Dublin

Peter Brady is an elected member of the prestigious World Master Chefs Society and regularly represents Ireland abroad at food fairs and competitions, as well as being executive chef in one of the leading Dublin hotels.

Marinated Pheasant Breasts with Raspberry and Chanterelle Sauces

4 pheasant supremes (½ breasts)
1 glass port wine
1 fl oz olive oil
salt and freshly ground black pepper
2 crushed cloves of garlic
1 oz fresh chanterelle mushrooms (sliced)

for the sauces:
⅓ pint fresh raspberry juice
⅓ pint pheasant glaze
¼ pint double cream
⅓ lb unsalted butter

garnish:
4 filo pastry baskets
4 ozs small-diced, cooked vegetables

Remove the breasts from a brace of pheasants. Place these (removed from the bone) to marinate in the port and olive oil seasoned with salt and black pepper. The legs and the carcase are simmered in 2 pints of good brown stock. Strain, reserve the flesh to be used again in a pie or terrine. Reduce the cooking broth to a thick glaze. Remove the breasts from the marinade and rub them all over with the crushed garlic. Brown them quickly in a pan and finish them in a hot oven, covered in foil, until just cooked. They should still be pink inside. This will take about 15-20 minutes at 190°C (375°F, Gas Mark 5). Slice the breasts onto a plate with the two sauces and the vegetable baskets.

The raspberry sauce is prepared by simply puréeing the fruit through a mouli-sieve. The chanterelle sauce is prepared by combining over heat, the juices from the roasted breasts, the glaze, the cream, the sliced chanterelle mushrooms. The sauce is enriched with the butter just before serving. Serve with finely diced cooked vegetables wrapped in buttered filo pastry baskets.

Oatmeal Sweet

1oz oatmeal
4oz golden syrup
½ pint fresh cream
1 tsp lemon juice
3 tsp Irish whiskey

Toast the oatmeal under the grill. Whip the cream. Warm the syrup and mix in the lemon juice and the whiskey. Fold this mixture into the cream, adding most of the toasted oatmeal. Spoon into serving classes and chill well. Just before serving, sprinkle each helping with some of the remaining oatmeal.

Wexford Strawberry Twill Baskets

2 lbs fresh strawberries
4 tubs natural yoghurt
1 glass Irish Mist liqueur
¼ red pepper
¼ yellow pepper
freshly ground black pepper

Hull the fresh strawberries and cut them in half. Macerate 1 lb in a little curaçao. Mix the other half with the yoghurt. Just before serving, mix the Irish Mist liqueur into the yoghurt and strawberry mixture. Pour this over the other strawberries. Garnish with the flesh of the red and yellow peppers which have been cut into a small dice. Two or three twists of freshly ground black pepper to season.

The Park Restaurant, Blackrock, Co. Dublin

Colm O'Daly, the chef-patron of The Park Restaurant, on the southern outskirts of Dublin, is one of the growing band of internationally recognised, young Irish chefs and was recently elected to the World Master Chefs Society. He established his reputation as the chef of the world-famous Park Hotel in Kenmare, Co Kerry, before opening his own restaurant in Blackrock with the success his innovative and reasonably priced fare deserves.

Roast Stuffed Loin of Lamb with Rhubarb and Mint

½ loin of lamb
1 lamb's kidney
lamb's caul
1 shallot
2 sticks young rhubarb
100 ml lamb stock
25 gm breadcrumbs
2 tbs madeira
2 tbs chopped fresh mint
1 oz butter
salt and freshly ground black pepper

Make the stuffing by frying the finely diced shallot in the butter with 1 tbs of the chopped fresh mint. Add one stick of the finely diced rhubarb. Season, mix through the breadcrumbs and allow to cool.

Remove the skin, bone and any excess fat from the loin of lamb, season with more of the chopped fresh mint, salt and pepper. Place the stuffing along the inside of the loin and fold over. Gently stretch the lamb's caul (membrane of fat) and wrap it round the loin, making sure that it is well sealed.

Skin and core the lamb's kidney and set it aside. On a hot pan seal the loin on all sides and place in a pre-heated moderate oven 180°C (365°F, Gas Mark 4-5) for 6-8 minutes. The flesh should be pink. Remove from the oven and allow to rest. Seal the kidney halves on a hot pan and allow to cook. Slice the remainder of the rhubarb and add to the pan. When the kidneys are firm, remove the kidney and deglaze the pan with the madeira. Add the lamb stock (made from the bones) and any juice from the loin. Season to taste.

Carve the lamb and serve on a warmed joint plate with the kidney. Strain on the sauce. Garnish with a bouquet of fresh mint.

Mincemeat Parcels with Cranberry Ice-cream

for the mincemeat parcels:
½ lb currants
¼ lb raisins
¼ lb sultanas
¼ lb chopped candied peel
2 oz chopped glacé cherries (optional)
¼ lb soft dark brown sugar
½ lb peeled, chopped apple
grated rind and juice of 1 lemon
¼ lb butter (melted)
¼ tsp mixed spice (level measure)
¼ tsp grated nutmeg (level measure)
¼ tsp ground cinnamon (level measure)
a good pinch of ground cloves
4 tbsp Irish whiskey or Irish Mist liqueur
1 lb filo pastry

for the Cranberry Ice-cream:
1 pint milk
6 egg yolks
6 oz sugar
1 pint whipping cream
12 oz cranberries
2 tsp lemon juice
4 oz sieved icing sugar

To make the mincemeat, mix the spices with the sugar, add the fruits and pour in the melted butter and the spirits. Mix very thoroughly. Put into clean, sealed jars and store for at least 14 days before using.

Cut the sheets of filo pastry into 3-inch (7.5 cm) squares and layer three or four squares with melted butter. Put a small tablespoonful of the mincemeat in the centre and shape the pastry like a draw-string purse, tying the top loosely with tape. Bake for 15-20 minutes in a hot oven at 200°C (400°F, gas mark 6).

For the ice-cream, make a custard with the milk, egg yolks and plain sugar. Cover and cool. Blend the cranberries, lemon juice and sieved icing sugar to a smooth purée and fold into the custard. Half-whip the cream and stir this into the custard mixture. Freeze as for any ice-cream, breaking up the crystals occasionally. Store in the freezer until required.

SOURCES

Agriculture & Fisheries, Dept. of. *Cookery Notes.*
    Dublin: Dept. of Agriculture & Fisheries.

Allen, Myrtle. *The Ballymaloe Cookbook.*
    Dublin: Agri-Books, 1977.

Barker, Philip. *Understanding Archaeological Excavation.*
    London: Batsford, 1986.

Barry, T. B. *The Archaeology of Medieval Ireland.*
    London: Methuen, 1987.

Berry, James. *Tales of Old Ireland.*
    London: Robinson Publishing, 1984.

Bord Iascaigh Mhara, An. *Fish From Irish Coastal Waters.*
    Dublin.

Bradby, Richard. *The Pre-historic Settlement of Britain.*
    London: Routledge & Kegan Paul Ltd.

Brown, Terence. *Ireland : A Social and Cultural History, 1922-79.*
    London: Fontana, 1981.

Buckley, Victor. *Curraghtarsna Fulucht Fiadh.*
    (Current Archaeology, No. 98)

Cadogan, Mary & Bond, Shirley. *The Oat Cookbook.*
    London: Martin Dunitz, 1987.

Cullen, L. M. *Life in Ireland.*
    London: Batsford, 1979.

Danaher, Kevin. *In Ireland Long Ago.*
    Cork: Mercier Press, 1962.

Danaher, Kevin. *Gentle Places and Simple Things.*
    Cork: Mercier Press, 1964.

Danaher, Kevin. *The Hearth and Stool and All.*
    Cork: Mercier Press, 1985.

Danaher, Kevin. *The Year in Ireland.*
    Cork: Mercier Press, 1972.

Davidson, Alan. *North Atlantic Seafood.*
    London: MacMillan.

Doherty, J.E. & Hickey, D. J. *A Chronology of Irish History Since 1500.* Dublin: Gill & Macmillan, 1989.

Drew, David & Huddart, David. *The Dunmore Cave.*
    Dublin: Irish Parks & Monuments Service.

Edwards, Ruth Dudley. *An Atlas of Irish History.*
London: Methuen, 1973.

Ellis, Peter Berresford. *Hell or Connaught.*
The Cromwellian Settlement of Ireland, 1662 - 1670.
London: Hamish Hamilton, 1975.

Evans, E. Estyn. *Irish Folk Ways.*
London: Routledge & Kegan Paul, 1979.

Evans, E. Estyn. *The Personality of Ireland.*
Belfast: Blackstaff Press, 1981.

FitzGibbon, Theodora. *Irish Traditional Food.*
London: Pan Books, 1984.

FitzGibbon, Theodora. *A Taste of Ireland.*
London: Dent, 1968.

FitzGibbon, Theodora. *The Food of The Western World.*
London: Hutchinson, 1976.

Flanagan, Lawrence. *Ireland's Armada Legacy.*
Dublin: Gill & MacMillan, 1988.

Gore, Lilian. *Game Cooking.*
London: Penguin Books, 1976.

Grigson, Geoffrey. *An Englishman's Flora.*
London: Paladin, 1975.

Hartley, Dorothy. *Food in England.*
London: McDonald, 1954.

Hurst, Bernice. *Bailey's Original Irish Cream*
Effortless Entertaining. London: Sphere, 1987.

Irish Countrywomen's Association. *Irish Countrywomen's*
Association Cookery Book. Dublin: 1978.

Irish Countrywomen's Association. *Irish Countrywomen's*
Association Cookery Book. Dublin: 1985.

Irwin, Florence. *The Cookin' Woman.*
Belfast: Blackstaff Press, 1986.

Johnson, Hugh. *The Story of Wine.*
London: Mitchell Beazley, 1989.

Johnston, James P. *A Hundred Years of Eating.*
Dublin: Gill & Macmillan, 1977.

Kavanagh, Peter. *A Guide to Irish Mythology.*
Athlone: Goldsmith Press, 1988.

Keane, John B. *Strong Tea.*
Cork: Mercier Press, 1963.

Keane, John B. *Owl Sandwiches.*
Tralee: Brandon Press, 1985.

Keane, Mary Angela. *The Burren* (Irish Heritage Series).
Dublin: Eason & Son, Ltd.

Knight, Denis [Editor]. *Cobbett in Ireland.*
London: Lawrence & Wishart, 1984.

Laverty, Maura & Le Brocquy, Sybil. *Kind Cooking.*
    Tralee: The Kerryman.
Logan, Patrick. *Irish Country Cures.*
    Belfast: Appletree Press, 1981.
Loughrey, Patrick [Editor]. *The People of Ireland.*
    Belfast: Appletree Press, 1988.
Luard, Elizabeth. *European Peasant Cookery.*
    London: Bantam Press, 1986.
Lucas, A. T. *Irish Food Before The Potato.*
    Gwerin, Volume III, No. 2., 1960.
Lucas, A.T. *Nettles and Charlock as a Famine Food.*
    Breifne Historical Society, Vol. I, No. 2.
MacLysaght, Edward. *Irish Life in the Seventeenth Century.*
    Dublin: Irish Academic Press, 1969.
Magee, Malachy. *One Thousand Years of Irish Whiskey.*
    Dublin: O'Brien Press, 1980.
McCracken, Eileen. *Irish Woods Since Tudor Times.*
    London: David & Charles, 1971.
Meyer, Kuno [Editor]. *Aislinge: The Vision of MacConglinne.*
    London: 1892.
Mitchell, Frank. *Reading the Irish Landscape.*
    London: Country House Books, 1986.
Moody, T. W. & Martin, F. X. *The Course of Irish History.*
    Cork: Mercier Press, 1967.
Myers, J. P. *Elizabethan Ireland.*
    London: Archon Press, 1983.
Nolan, William [Editor]. *The Shaping of Ireland.*
    RTE Thomas Davis Lectures. Cork: Mercier Press, 1986.
Ó Céirín, Cyril & Kit. *Wild & Free.*
    Dublin: O'Brien Press, 1986.
O'Farrell, Padraig. *Gems of Irish Wisdom.*
    Cork: Mercier Press, 1980.
O'Kelly, M.J. & C. *Guide to Lough Gur.*
    Dublin: Claire O'Kelly, 1978.
O'Leary, Peter. *My Story.*
    Oxford: Oxford University Press, 1987.
O'Meara, John J [Editor & trans.] Wales, Gerald of.
    The History and Topography of Ireland.
    London: Penguin Books,1982.
Phillips, Roger. *Wild Food.*
    London: Pan, 1983.
Phillips, Patricia. *The Pre-history of Europe.*
    London: Allen Lane.
Powell, T.G.E. *The Celts.*
    London: Thames & Hudson Ltd.

Praeger, Robert Lloyd. *Natural History of Ireland.*
London: E.P. Publishing.

Praeger, Robert Lloyd. *The Way That I Went.*
Dublin: Allen Figgis.

Ross, Dr. Ann. & Cyprien, Michael. *A Traveller's Guide to Celtic Britain.* London: Routledge & Kegan Paul, 1985.

Rowley, Trevor. *The Norman Heritage.*
London: Routledge & Kegan, 1983.

Scott, Michael [Editor]. *Hall's Ireland.*
London: Sphere, 1976.

Smyth, Daragh. *A Guide to Irish Mythology.*
Dublin: Irish Academic Press, 1988.

Somerville-Large, Peter. *Dublin.*
London: Granada, 1981.

Somerville-Large, Peter. *From Bantry Bay to Leitrim.*
London: Arena, 1986.

St. Canice's Cathedral, Kilkenny. *Cookery & Cures of Old Kilkenny.* Kilkenny: Boethius Press, 1983.

Stobart, Tom. *The Cook's Encyclopaedia.*
London: Cameron & Taylour, 1980.

Stobart, Tom. *Herbs, Spices and Flavourings.*
London: Penguin Books.

Taylor, Gordon. *A Handful of Herbs.*
London: Blond & Briggs, 1976.

Wallace, Patrick. *Aspects of Viking Dublin. Vols. 1 - 6.*
Dublin: Irish Life Assurance Co.

Woodman, Peter C. *The Post Glacial Settlement of Northern Europe.*

Claire Cotter [Editor], *Excavations 1985.*
Dublin: Irish Academic Publications.

INDEX OF RECIPES

Bread
Brown soda bread 61
Buttermilk for bread
making 66
Griddle bread 62
Oat bread 57
Wheat bread 60
White soda bread 62

Cake and Biscuit
Arbutus Lodge chocolate
gâteau 157
Brack 64
Buttermilk drop scones 40
Buttermilk scones 64
Curranty cake 63
Kerry apple cake 67
Oat and wheat biscuits 59
Oat cakes 58
Pancakes 40
Porter cake 68
Potato pastry 135
Pratie apples 133
Tea brack 65
Treacle bread and scones 64

Cheese
Buttermilk cheese 41
Buttermilk cream curd 42
Quark-type cheese 42

Drink
Hot whiskey 145
Irish coffee 148
Mulled ale 145
Posset cup 146
Scáiltín 146
Sloe gin 147

Fish
Baked (whole) salmon 12
Barbecued (whole) salmon
11
Boiled ling 20
Drimcong steamed brill in
carrot sauce 161
Eel 15
Fried herring in oatmeal 18
Herrings 16
Killybegs herrings 17
Ling 20
Lough Neagh fried eels 15
Mackerel 19
Salmon 11
Sea, white, salmon trout 14
Smoked salmon 14

Meat & Game
An Irish breakfast 104
Arbutus Lodge forester's pie
156
Bacon and cabbage 95
Baked ham 96
Ballymaloe Dingle pie 152
Beef 106
Beef stew 112
Bodices 106
Brawn 100
Clifford's gourmet Irish
stew 159

Clifford's warm black
    pudding salad 158
Collared fat ribs of beef 110
Corned beef and cabbage 107
Cruibeens 97
Drisheen 102
Dublin coddle 99
Goose 115
Grouse 86
Hare with sauce Irlandaise 87
Irish stew 114
Jury's Hotel marinated
    pheasant breasts with
    raspberry and
    chanterelle sauces 162
Lamb 113
Mutton 113
Park Hotel roast stuffed
    loin of lamb with
    rhubarb and mint 165
Pickled pork 97
Pigeon 86
Pork and bacon 94
Rabbit 89
Rabbit stew with bacon
    dumplings 89
Roast hare 87
Skirts and kidneys 105
Spiced beef 109
Tripe and onions 98
Venison 90

Milk
Buttermilk 39
Buttermilk curds 40
Buttermilk for bread
    making 66
Buttermilk plant 66
Cream 43
Cultured milk 39
Curds & whey 42
Thick milk 37
Troander 37
White stirabout 38
Yoghurt 39

Oat
Oat Bread 57
Porridge 55
Sloke and oatmeal cakes 56
White breakfast pudding 56

Potato
Boiled 123
Boxty 127
Boxty bread 128-30
Cally 124
Champ 124
Colcannon 126
Pandy 124
Potato cakes 130
Potato pastry 135
Potato soups 131
Potato stuffing 134
Poundies 124
Stampy 124

Pudding
Ballymaloe carrageen moss
    pudding 154
Buttermilk cheese and
    strawberries 41
Carrageen blancmange 38
Drimcong apples in red
    wine 161
Hallowe'en pudding 69
Irish cream liqueur granita
    143
Irish mist soufflé 144
Jury's Hotel oatmeal sweet
    163
Jury's Hotel Wexford straw-
    berry twill baskets 164
Mincemeat parcels with
    cranberry ice-cream 166

Sauce
Caramel sauce 154
Carrot sauce 161
Cream and sorrel sauce 13
Game sauce 92

Gooseberry sauce 19
Green mayonnaise 13
Irish coffee sauce 154
Mustard sauce 108
Onion sauce 104
Rowan jelly 93
Sauce Irlandaise 87

Shellfish
Ballymaloe dressed crab 151
Crayfish 26
Dublin Bay prawns 26
*Dublin Bay prawns flamed
    in Irish whiskey* 26
Lobster 26
Mussel 22
Mussels with wine 23
Oyster 21
Scallops 26

Soup
Arbutus Lodge nettle soup
    156
Bacon, pea and barley soup
    72
Carrageen winkles 24
Drimcong oyster broth 160
Kale soup 71
Leek and oatmeal soup 70
Nettle soup 71, 131
Potato soup 132
Watercress soup 132

Vegetable
Baked onions 74
Cabbage 75
Dillisk 26
Dulse 26
Kale 71
Leek 70
Mushrooms 76
Mushrooms in cream 77
Nettle 71
Onion 73
Onions in milk 74
Seakale 76
Seaweed 24
Sloke 25
Sloke and oatmeal cakes 56
Strange Irish salad 77

A Strange Kind of Loving

by Sheila Mooney

A touching, searingly honest and at times heartbreaking account of an upbringing in an Ascendancy family and the author's vain attempts to win the love and approval of her Victorian father while continuing to support her beautiful, eccentric and alcoholic mother. Sheila Mooney is the sister of 1930s Hollywood idol, Maureen O'Sullivan, and her memoir contains witty and illuminating accounts of her career.

POOLBEG

Women Surviving
Studies in the History of Irish Women in the 19th and 20th centuries

Edited by

Maria Luddy and Cliona Murphy

This highly original collection of historical articles addresses aspects of women's history in nineteenth and early twentieth-century Ireland, including: nuns in society; paupers and prostitutes; the impact of international feminists on the Irish suffrage movement and women's contribution to post-Independence Irish politics.

POOLBEG

The Poolbeg Golden Treasury of Well Loved Poems

Edited by Sean McMahon

By the compiler of *Rich and Rare*
and
The Poolbeg Book of Children's Verse

A delightful anthology of everyone's favourite poems, from Shakespeare to Patrick Kavanagh

POOLBEG